DO YOU FEEL ALONE IN THE SPIRIT?

Do You Feel
Alone in the Spirit?

Ruth Sanford

Servant Books
Ann Arbor, Michigan

Published by Servant Books
        Box 8617
        Ann Arbor, Michigan 48107

Available from: Distribution Center
        237 North Michigan
        South Bend, Indiana 46601

Scripture quotations in this book are taken from the
GOOD NEWS BIBLE—Old Testament: Copyright
© American Bible Society 1976; New Testament:
Copyright © American Bible Society 1966, 1971,
1976

Printed in the United States of America

ISBN 0-89283-056-5

CONTENTS

PREFACE

After Jesus' torture and crucifixion, his apostles—afraid of the Jews, fearful and unsure of the direction they should be taking—hid together in an upper room in Jerusalem. Jesus appeared to them there and said, "Receive my peace." And for all time Jesus has offered this same peace to everyone who would accept him.

If you have accepted Jesus as Lord of your life and have been filled with his Holy Spirit, then you have had a taste of that peace which only Jesus can give. But if you are a married woman and do not see your husband responding to Jesus in the ways you do, you may be without peace. You may feel that you and your husband are not one, that you are travelling different roads, that there can never be complete peace between you. Yet Jesus' offer is meant for you, now, even in a divisive marital situation.

I would like to share with you how I learned to receive the peace of Jesus, although my husband and I seemed to be going in different directions. I would like to tell you how Jesus showed me that I was not allowing him to be fully Lord of my life, Lord of my marriage. I made so many mistakes and experienced so much frustration and confusion until I learned to follow Jesus' plan for wives.

I hope that what I have learned through my own mistakes and through the Lord's patient correction can help you to see and accept the peace which Jesus wants so much for you right now.

ONE

MY TESTIMONY

I grew up in a small Connecticut town as the youngest of three girls. My parents were devout Catholics, who brought us up to have a deep faith in God. I can still remember my father leading us in night prayers and the reverence I felt during Mass on Sunday mornings. My religion appealed to me very much. I knew that I could talk to God and that he would listen to me.

Later, however, when I left home to attend a small Catholic women's college, I began to rebel against everything. I felt that God was either powerless or did not care about me, so I drifted away from the values of my childhood. I spent my time partying and began to profess agnosticism.

Early in the summer following my freshman year, I received a strange letter from my roommate Teresa, who had been my companion in rebellion. Teresa told me that she had just gotten involved in something called the "charismatic renewal": she had given her life to the Lord, had been "baptized in the Spirit," and was able to pray in tongues! I did not know exactly what to make of this. I was both intrigued and skeptical.

That fall, I hurried to my dorm to meet Teresa. I breathed a sigh of relief when I saw her: she at least looked the same. And she laughed and joked as much as ever. But when I tried to make plans to go partying as we had before, I quickly discovered that she had become a very different person.

Teresa told me what had happened to her during the summer—how she had encountered the Lord and formed a new, more personal relationship with him. Although I was impressed in many ways—she had obviously found something very fulfilling—my own first response was that I wanted no part of it. Yet the Lord set to work in me through the influence of Teresa. Within two months, I had finally faced my need to repent of the way I was living. I, too, then experienced an outpouring of God's Spirit.

My new relationship with the Lord changed me in many ways. Russ Sanford, an occasional date during my sophomore and junior years, decided that he liked those changes. By the end of my junior year, we were engaged.

As we entered into our marriage, I, like most brides, viewed our future with optimism. We seemed to have everything going for us. I felt that I had grown up in the Lord a lot over the last year and a half, and I knew that Russ was a strong man and a dedicated Catholic. In fact, I used to say I was marrying him because I couldn't wrap him around my little finger. We had clear goals, good friends, and were very much in love, but I was totally unprepared for the reality that hit when we returned from our honeymoon. Russ did not see the need to make many of the adjustments I assumed would be part of our marriage. While we had many happy times and warm, shared experiences, I was often confused and unhappy. More and more, I put all my hopes for our marriage on getting Russ into the charismatic renewal.

At the time, we were living in South Bend, Indiana, where Russ was in law school. I was attending the meetings of a local prayer group, but Russ felt that he did not have the time to get involved in the charismatic renewal—even though he sensed that God might be offering him a deeper spiritual life. He kept promising the

Lord that when he had time, he would take a closer look at all of this.

I didn't know that. All I knew was that Russ never showed any interest in the prayer group. I preached at him, I pleaded with him, I cajoled him. I left charismatic literature laying around the house, hoping he would pick something up and be convinced by it. I would share with him all the teaching from the prayer meeting that I thought he needed to hear; I desperately tried to get him to meet my friends from the prayer group. I got to the point where I was thinking of him as a pagan who needed conversion, when in fact he remained a good Christian all along. I began to wonder whether I should ever have married him. In short, I was making myself miserable.

My hopes for Russ's "conversion" disappeared when he decided we should move to Massachusetts after his graduation from law school. Away from the group in South Bend, I felt, he would never be baptized in the Spirit. As it turned out, it was while we were in the east that the Lord finally began to deal with the real problems in our marriage.

Soon after we arrived in Massachusetts, I felt a prompting from the Lord that *I* was the obstacle to Russ's being baptized in the Spirit. At first, I was insulted by this idea, but during the next months, I began to see the truth in it. I had found a small group of women involved in the charismatic renewal, and was meeting with them regularly for fellowship. Out of these meetings came the gradual realization that I might not be as holy as I thought I was. With their help, I began to see ways that I needed to change my attitudes toward Russ and his spiritual development.

Meanwhile, life in the east was not working out the way Russ had expected. He found his job frustrating and felt that it was leading nowhere. Our finances were in terrible shape. We could not move into the house we had rented because the builders were not finished, so we had to rent an apartment at very high rates. After six months, we moved to another town in an attempt to improve our finances. Unknown to me, Russ promised the Lord that if this move did not work out well, we would go back to South Bend.

Since I did not know exactly what Russ was thinking throughout these difficulties, I saw the new move as yet another setback. Away from the support of my fellowship group, I quickly sank back into self-pity. Russ's job continued to go badly; on top of that, I became sick, we had rats in our house, and our relationship was suffering. "Why can't Russ see what God's doing?" I wondered. "Doesn't he realize that nothing is going to go right until he gets his spiritual life in order?"

That was still my attitude one day when I was reading an article that discussed the book of Job. The author recounted all the evils that befell Job. At each point I nodded and thought, "Oh, yes, that's me. I'm just like Job. A righteous woman suffering through no fault of her own." I slowly slumped deeper into my self-pity. But the end of the article was a shock.

"Do you know what Job's real problem was?" the author asked. "Pride! Job thought he could stand by himself for God's sake, instead of humbly begging for strength from God."

Pride?! Could it actually be, that at the heart of all my misery lay my own pride? Suddenly I saw that despite all the Lord had shown me about my own sins and bad attitudes, I was still concentrating on how I wanted Russ to change—not on the changes I needed to make. In my pride, I was blaming Russ for all our problems and blaming God for Russ.

"Dear Father in heaven," I prayed, "please help me. I don't think I can stand this anymore. I need you, Lord. Show me what you want me to do."

For three days, I cried with sorrow for the pride and stubbornness God had shown me. But at the end of that time, I could feel the Lord's strength flow into me. I knew that he had forgiven me, and was going to help me change.

It was amazing how quickly God worked once my pride was out of the way. Little more than a week after my change of heart, Russ told me that he felt we should move back to South Bend and join the prayer group, which had since become a more committed community. He told me what he had been thinking during all those months when things were going badly. He told me how he had felt that the Lord might be offering him something in the charismatic renewal, and explained why he had held back.

Russ was baptized in the Spirit soon after our return to South Bend. In the years since, we both have had many growing pains, but we have seen the Lord constantly strengthen our relationship with each other and with him.

Today, as I look back on those first four years of my marriage, I can see more clearly both my mistakes and the truths that helped turn me in the right direction. In this book, I want to share these lessons with you. Whether your husband is a good Christian who does not share your involvement in something like the charismatic renewal, or not a Christian at all, you may experience the same discouragement, loneliness, and frustration that I felt—the sense that you are alone in the Spirit.

But you are *not* alone. If you have the Spirit, you have God himself with you in everything. You also have many sisters who can support you with their fellowship and encouragement. And—what is often overlooked—you have your husband. For no matter what your husband's Christian commitment, your marriage to him is a relationship blessed and backed by God. Through your wedding vows, God joined you to this man. He made him your protector and head. He promises to honor this relationship and use it to give you strength, but you may need to learn how to cooperate with him. In the next chapters, I want to talk about the way a wife's attitudes toward her husband can affect what God is able to accomplish through their relationship.

TWO

LETTING GO

Picture a couple climbing a steep, rocky mountain, with Jesus in the lead. Jesus is clearly confident of the footing, for he walks with a sure step, even though he is walking backward to face the couple. The wife is next in line and is holding tightly to Jesus' hand. Her other hand, however, is grasping tightly to her husband who is further down the slope. The wife's arms are completely stretched as she tries to hold on to both Jesus and her husband. She is facing her husband, urging him along. As one watches the procession, it becomes clear that the husband cannot even see Jesus on the path ahead because of his wife blocking the view. He seems reluctant to continue, which is why his wife keeps trying to urge him along; but because she is looking backward, she keeps slipping and falling. She is obviously in pain.

This is a picture of a wife who is holding on to her husband's spiritual life. She is afraid that if she lets go, her husband will slide down the mountain and perish. From my own experience and from what I have seen happening with my friends, I have realized that holding on is one of the basic mistakes a woman can make when she is involved in the charismatic renewal without her husband.

Holding on is an attitude of heart that makes a wife act as if she alone were responsible for saving her husband and bringing him into a relationship with Jesus. She acts as if she herself were the Holy Spirit, trying to touch her husband's heart in such a way that he accepts full life in the Lord.

On the practical level, this wife might come home from a prayer meeting talking excitedly about everything that went on, not thinking how strange it sounds to her husband.

She might be sure to mention other men who were at the meeting, hoping her husband will come because of them.

She might repeat a teaching because she thinks her husband should incorporate it into his life.

She might recommend books for her husband to read or leave them laying by his favorite chair.

She might leave a Christian magazine opened to a certain article, hoping her husband will read it.

She might beg him to attend prayer meetings with her, perhaps even pointing out areas in which, she feels, her husband obviously needs the saving power of Jesus.

She might start inviting Christian friends over to dinner, hoping their evangelizing will work when her own has failed.

If we have done any of these things, we have been holding on to our husbands. Yet there are also more subtle ways to hold on to our husbands. They can be just as hard on our relationship.

We are probably holding on if we see almost everything in terms of how it will affect our husbands. For example, our *initial* response to prophecy or teaching at a prayer meeting may be, "Oh, I wish John had been here to hear that," or "Lord, could you somehow teach the same thing to John, even though he's not here?"

We are holding on if we receive a Scripture passage in prayer and immediately try to think of some way to share it with our husbands.

We are holding on when we try to present some word from the Lord to our husbands as a general sharing, when we actually believe it was tailor-made for their ears.

My own experience with holding on was that I would rarely try to persuade Russ to come to prayer meetings or attend conferences, but my heart was not at peace concerning him. With my lips, I could entrust him to Jesus, but at the same time I would wish and wish for a change in him. I found it very difficult to accept Russ's relationship with God the way it was. And although I never expressed these feelings to Russ, it was impossible for him not to feel their effects in a relationship as close as marriage.

At times, I was beset by fears. Would my relationship with Jesus ruin my relationship with Russ? Would it make us grow further apart? Had I made a mistake in choosing my husband? Would we ever be "one" in approaching the Lord? Although I tried to deny the existence of these fears, they would float in and out of my life, causing more anxiety and more tension in my relationship with Russ.

In short, the whole problem of holding on is complicated by many emotions in both of the partners. A husband often fears that his wife's relationship with Jesus will divide them. He is not used to sharing his wife's love and does not always understand that her love for the Lord will result in greater love between the two of them. He may also be confused by the swiftness with which she forms close attachments to new Christian friends. Even if he sees these relationships as good for her, he may be afraid that he will get pressured into them himself.

Probably the greatest threat a husband faces, however, is the idea that his own relationship with God might not be adequate. He might need to change, and change hurts. We grow up in a society that claims many victims to depression, nervous breakdowns, and broken relationships. If we have managed to survive and lead a fairly normal life, we are careful to protect ourselves from any force that might rock the boat.

If, on top of this, a wife presents the charismatic renewal to her husband as the "right" way to live, the logical conclusion seems to be that she thinks her husband is living all wrong. That would not only be hard for him to accept and deal with, it is usually the wrong way to present people with the good news of all Jesus has for us.

When any of these factors is at work in your marriage, the effect is to back your husband into a corner. He grows very defensive or suspicious of your actions. Remember our image of the couple struggling on the mountain. The husband does not really want to go up the mountain. But from his vantage point, his fight is with his wife. He cannot even see the Lord. His wife needs to step aside and let go. Any wife who is not at peace in her marriage because of her husband's relationship with God needs to let go, to allow Jesus himself to lead her husband. She should approach her husband tenderly with total acceptance and love centered in Jesus.

That sounds fine in theory, but what about in practice? How can we relinquish our anxiety over our husband's spiritual life and release him to the care of the Lord? How can we "let go" of our husbands enough to love them more completely and accept them for who they are?

First, we need to realize that Jesus died in order that our husbands might receive salvation. He loves our husbands more than we do. We need to reflect upon that fact until we really believe it.

Secondly, our husbands' relationships with Jesus, while they affect us as their wives, are nevertheless exclusively between Jesus and our husbands. No amount of wishing, hoping, or anxiety can change the fact that we cannot carry our husbands along by our own spirituality. The relationship between God and any person is totally a work of the Spirit. We are out of order if we are trying to manipulate our husbands into a relationship with God.

Let's return to the mountain imagery. Suppose the wife stops trying to pull her husband along and steps back on the path to stand beside him. She is now free to turn around and face Jesus. And because she is no longer being pulled in two directions, she is more relaxed and peaceful. Her husband, meanwhile, is now able to see Jesus calling him up the mountain and offering him his hand. The love of Jesus can draw the husband to climb the path. When he stumbles, it is Jesus who reaches out for him.

Once we realize that we need to let Jesus lead our husbands, we must decide to let go of our anxiety about them. We have to go before the Father and pray earnestly for the grace to do this. We must constantly turn to the Lord for help when we begin to grow anxious. We need to ask the Father to take care of our husbands, to lead them according to his plan, to give them the joy of knowing Jesus more closely, to make them the men the Lord would have them be. Remember, God loves our husbands enough to give them a free will; we should love them that much, too. We should keep our eyes on Jesus, eager to obey his word to us without trying to coerce our husbands into holiness.

After making this decision and praying for God's grace to stick to it, we must begin to act accordingly. I described earlier the wrong way to react to words of prophecy or Scripture; now I would like to mention more appropriate responses. As we hear or read a word from God, we should stand before him in humility and ask him to open our hearts to receive and understand what he is saying. We should expect that God is speaking to us—not to our husbands—unless a prophecy is explicitly directed toward someone different or unless we have asked God to give us a passage for someone in particular.

In most cases, we should not share in detail about what happens at the prayer meeting. If what happens there helps us become more loving, that is what our husbands will be interested in.

If our husbands have reservations about our Christian activities, we should try to answer their questions candidly, without defensiveness. It is right for our husbands to question us about the things we are involved in. If we cannot answer all their questions, we should simply say, "I don't know." If they mention something that has also been troubling us, we should say so. No prayer group or community or parish that I know has reached perfection yet. It would be foolish to try to hide a group's faults. Further discussion with a mature member of the group may help answer both our husbands' questions and our own.

Sometimes we should share with our husbands about the things we are learning from the Lord, but in doing so, we must be very sensitive to the Lord's timing. We should pray daily with the psalmist, "Lord, place a guard at my mouth, a sentry at the door of my lips" (Ps. 141:3). The Lord will honor our prayer and keep us from speaking when we should not. He will also open our mouths when we should speak.

I can recall times when I wanted so much to share with Russ some insights I had received. The words were right there ready to come pouring out of my mouth, but it was as if my mouth was glued shut. It was really comical. After struggling to speak for a minute or so, I would be reminded of that prayer I often prayed. I would then thank God for helping me.

At other times, the opposite would happen. I would not be particularly in the mood to share about the Lord, but the Lord would urge me to speak. The words were always right there.

What do we do, though, when we are so filled with joy at the end of a prayer meeting or at the end of a day when we have felt close to Jesus that we want to grab our husbands as they walk in the door and share and share and share? Most of the time we should resist the urge. We can praise God on our way home from a meeting or thank and praise him in our homes all day. We are free to share with Christian sisters. But our husbands are not going to want to hear all about our spiritual lives right after a full day of their own. They need to know of our love and concern for them as they come home from work. And when we come home from meetings, remember our husbands have been without us, possibly alone or babysitting to allow us to attend. Let's come in and show that we want to be with them. We can do something extra to serve and love them—fixing a snack, offering a back rub, bringing a cup of coffee. Let's allow the love and joy we experience in Jesus to flow over into our relationship with our husbands.

These are all things I began to learn and do as I "let go" of my husband. I did not change overnight. It was a slow process and even now I occasionally feel myself trying to hold on again. But I have gradually learned that when I begin to be anxious or unpeaceful, I am slipping into my old patterns of relating. I then take my anxiety to the Lord in prayer, crying out to him for help.

At times I would become very upset because I would struggle with my anxiety for days without apparent change. I was afraid that my inability to accept Russ as he was would block him from ever allowing the Spirit of God to pour into his life.

I learned, however, that the Lord honored even my struggles. He was the one who had drawn Russ and I together, and he saw to it that my inadequacies would not damage Russ's relationship with him. Besides, I did not really have my eyes fixed on Russ at those times; I had them focused on myself. I would be bogged down in guilt or self pity until I looked up and saw the Lord. Then I could repent, put my eyes back on Jesus, and find the strength to act properly.

This is a gradual process. At times it seems impossible to let go and continue to grow in love for Jesus and our husbands. But there is encouragement in Scripture:

> Now that we have been put right with God through faith, we have peace with God through our Lord Jesus Christ. He has brought us by faith into this experience of God's grace, in which we now live. And so we boast of the hope we have of sharing God's glory! We also boast of our troubles, because we know that trouble produces endurance, endurance brings God's approval, and his approval creates hope. This hope does not disappoint us, for God has poured out his love into our hearts by means of the Holy Spirit, who is God's gift to us.

> Rom. 5:1–5

Simple and fervent devotion to Jesus is our protection in a hard situation. We cannot do anything without the Spirit living in us, working through us, praying through us, talking through us. But the Spirit is a free gift. We need only to accept the fact that Jesus loves us, and let him become the Lord of our lives. So, if anything I say seems impossible, remember that Jesus makes all things possible.

I know many women who have experienced God's peace in their marriages after they let go of their husbands in some of the ways I have described. I remember one woman in particular, whom I will call Lynn.

Lynn's marriage seemed a disaster after only nine months. Her husband was seriously considering a divorce. He was not a baptized Christian, but had consented to a marriage in Lynn's church. Lynn had a sporadic relationship with God before her marriage and had attended prayer meetings irregularly. She had not sought God's will about her marriage, and had married Ken against the advice of many friends. Their life together proved difficult from the start, and it kept going downhill fast.

Lynn gradually stopped attending church and prayer meetings. I met her eight months later. She had finally realized how wrong she had been to run rebelliously into the marriage, but she also knew the marriage was a covenant made before God.

"I've made my bed. Now I've got to lie in it," she told me at our first meeting. She did not know how far she had come just by accepting her marriage rather than looking for an out. Her biggest desire was that Ken come to know Jesus. She was resolved to try to evangelize him or get him to a prayer meeting.

We talked quite a bit that day about holding on and letting go, but Lynn was wary of the whole idea. I assured her that if she would begin, she could be at peace in her marriage and even experience deep joy.

I was very surprised the next day when Lynn called me.

She said, "I went home last night and asked Ken's forgiveness for nagging him so much, and told him that he had been right about telling me I should do what he wants in the house instead of pointing out the way other husbands act. I didn't promise big changes, but, you know, you were right. I haven't felt this much peace or joy in my whole married life, not even the day I walked down the aisle."

Ken was taken off guard by Lynn's new behavior. He was suspicious for a while because Lynn had already been through many ups and downs. But as Lynn continued to change and grow, he began to respond to her. He started by buying her some things he knew she liked. Then he began to ask her questions about God. Lynn knew she did not have all the answers, but responded as best she could. At this time, Ken has not even felt drawn to go to church or a prayer meeting, but he no longer talks about a divorce and is beginning to show pride in his wife. For her part, Lynn still has some difficult times, but she is at peace, knowing they are both in the hands of the Lord Jesus.

Another woman I know had a fairly good relationship with her husband, but often felt tense and irritable with him. Ann's husband was a strong member of his church and even attended prayer meetings regularly. But she was not satisfied with Jim the way he was. He had mentioned that he wanted to get up every morning at 6:30 to pray. In reality, he did well to be up on time for work at 8:30. Ann herself was up at 6:30 each day. She wanted very much for Jim to take a prayer time, so she would faithfully call him to get up. As it grew later, she would be more and more tense. "Why can't he get up?" she would think to herself. "He's had enough sleep and he's going to miss his prayer time. I know he needs that time so badly. When he doesn't pray he gets so depressed."

One morning she had already called Jim twice and resented having to call him again. She was preparing to go upstairs and tell Jim how aggravated she was when the Lord seemed to speak to her heart.

"Why do you think you are tense and Jim's days are getting harder? By the time Jim gets up you are so angry that it takes all his strength just to be civil when he reaches work."

Ann thought about this a minute, then began preparing breakfast for Jim. She placed it on a tray, added a note telling of her love for him, and took it up to him. Jim's response surprised her—he asked her to bring over his shirt and trousers, too! Ann did that, and the two had a good time talking before Jim left for work. He had been feeling a need for his wife to show some extra concern.

Not only did Ann's actions help her relationship with her husband, but Jim got much better about appearing at the table by at least 7:30, knowing he wouldn't be greeted by a crabby wife. Ann's whole days are now less tense. She no longer frets and grows irritable if Jim sleeps in. She simply does her morning work, calls for him regularly, and happily greets him when he does wake up. Although she occasionally slips into resentment or anger, she is learning to renounce it quickly and ask for God's grace to serve her husband joyfully.

This is not an easy way to live, but we follow one whose cross was not easy. He led the way in showing us how to lay down our lives in love. He won for us the power to be victorious in our own lives. When we are in the center of God's will, we not only endure, we share in the peace and joy and triumph of God.

THREE

RESPECT

*Love must be completely sincere. Hate what
is evil, hold on to what is good. Love one
another warmly as Christian brothers, and
be eager to show respect for one another.*
                                    Rom. 12:9–10

In these verses, Paul explains how we should relate
to one another in the body of Christ. We find it easy
to follow his instructions as we meet with our Christian
brothers and sisters at church or at the prayer meeting.
We greet the prayer meeting leader with respect. We
have a great respect for those who helped lead us into
a new relationship with Jesus. Our very manner with
them indicates our esteem. We find any faults in these
brothers and sisters easy to forgive.

On the other hand, we may have trouble feeling
much esteem for our husbands. We are very conscious
of all the differences between the way they act and the
way our new brothers and sisters act. If only they felt as
we do about the Lord, we think, all our problems would
be over.

This is, I believe, a very common experience for a
woman who is involved in the charismatic renewal
when her husband is not. She has only limited opportu-
nities for fellowship with others who share her experience of the Lord, so she tends to see those people
through rose-colored glasses. The contrast makes her

husband's faults seem even more glaring. One could almost say that it is easy to honor the brother and sister we do not live with, but hard to honor the brothers we do live with—our husbands.

Yet Scripture tells us clearly that we are to respect our husbands: ". . . every wife must respect her husband" (Eph. 5:33). Scripture does not add qualifiers—"Show respect if your husband is prayerful" or "Respect him if you agree with him." It is hard sometimes to show great respect for someone we know as well as our husbands. But Jesus asks us to do this.

Jesus himself respects our husbands. He has enough respect for them never to force them to do anything. He allows them their free will. He offers forgiveness for every wrong they commit. He was even nailed to a cross for their sake. If Jesus loves and respects our husbands that much, can we do less?

Sometimes, we do not want to admit that we do not always respect our husbands. Yet I doubt that there is a wife living who does not at times feel disrespectful of her husband. We may cringe with visible embarrassment when our husbands behave in some way we dislike, or ridicule them in front of others, or dominate conversations because we think they sound foolish.

There is a very fine line between feeling disrespect and showing it. It is important, then, that we feel respect for our husbands, that we fill our hearts with esteem for the men God has bound us to.

I myself have found disrespect to be near the core of difficulties in any relationship, especially my relationship with my husband. If I lose respect for Russ, how can I love him as I should? If our husbands do not have a committed relationship with Jesus, we should ask the Holy Spirit to show us whether we lack respect for them in their present spiritual state. If we do, we need to ask the Lord to forgive us and to put a deep, abiding respect for them into our hearts.

Please note, I am not saying you have to agree with your husband in everything or think every attitude he has is right. You must simply respect his uniqueness enough to allow him to be himself. If the truth were told, people could probably find a few imperfections in us, too. But we certainly want love and respect for ourselves.

The letter to the Ephesians says that wives are to submit to their husbands "as to the Lord" (5:22). That carries over to the respect we should have for them. It is overwhelming to think that we owe our husbands the same respect we owe the Lord—even if our marriage has serious problems or a particular husband does not "deserve" respect. None of us deserves the great outpouring of love Jesus has for us.

In determining where my heart is in relation to respecting my husband, I find it helpful to look at a specific day and review in my mind every encounter with my husband during that day. Would I have acted and reacted the same way if that were Jesus who had trouble getting out of bed? If that were Jesus who did not notice my special effort to make a good breakfast? If that were Jesus who came home from work tired and dragging? If that were Jesus who wanted to read the newspaper when I wanted to talk?

You may object, "But Jesus wouldn't do those irritating things." Maybe not. But Jesus does not say to respect our husbands only when they act as he does. We are to show respect out of reverence for Christ, who has established our marriages.

Let's take a look at what respect for our husbands can mean practically. Have you ever heard a conversation like this?

Wife: "What's the matter?"

Husband: "Nothing."

Ten minutes later, the wife repeats, "What's the matter, Honey?"

"Nothing!"

"Something's wrong. I can tell. What is it?"

"Nothing's wrong. Forget it."

"You can tell me. I'm your wife."

"Nothing's wrong," the husband says again. And with that he walks out of the room, leaving his wife in tears of frustration and rage.

What is really happening in that conversation? Why would a husband exclude his wife at a time when he is obviously troubled? Let's take a closer look.

When the wife asks, "What's the matter?" she indicates her assurance that she can see her husband is troubled. His "Nothing" indicates unwillingness to communicate. Repeating this exchange only pushes him further into isolation. The final appeal, "You can tell me, I'm your wife," may sound loving, but is really an attack. The wife is saying that her husband is wrong for not communicating, that he owes it to her to share everything that is on his mind at the moment he is thinking about it. When he responds to that attack by leaving the room, all possibility of communication ends. The wife is left feeling frustrated because she thought she was being nice in encouraging her husband to share his inmost soul.

A more helpful way to handle this kind of conversation is to recognize that your husband may sometimes need to be left alone. Many people need time to work out problems by themselves. You yourself probably need breathing room with the house quiet and the kids out of the way. Your husband needs breathing room, too. If you can see that he is troubled, ask Jesus to guide his thoughts before you say anything to him yourself.

While giving your husband breathing room, you can let him know that you are supporting him. In fact, he may want to talk with you about the problem if he is not knocked down before he starts. Here is my alternative to "What's the matter?"

"Gee, love, you look as if you've got something on your mind. Here's a cup of coffee; why don't you go sit in the other room and relax? If you'd like to talk I'll be in here, but if not, I just want you to know I love you."

That lets him know you are concerned without putting any pressure on him. Often, someone who is troubled does not even know what is wrong. That is one reason why "What's the matter?" can be so damaging. If your husband cannot put his finger on whatever is wrong, he will only be more frustrated by your questioning.

My husband has always been big on solitary walks. The first few times this happened, I gasped as he closed the door. I would wait up for him, crying, worrying, praying. Gradually, I learned that he needed this outlet. I got so I would notice him getting agitated or thoughtful, and say, "Should I get your coat?" Or sometimes he would say he was going out for cigarettes, and I would laugh and ask, "Should I wait up?"

Know your husband. Whatever is a sign to you that he may need to be alone, respect it. Do not act as if he is wronging you, but let him know that you love him and are willing to talk if he wants that.

Forgiveness is also tied in with respect. If you are holding some sort of grudge against another person, you cannot feel real respect for him. So when you notice that you are harboring resentment against your husband, confess it to the Lord, repent, and pray for your husband and yourself. You cannot afford an unforgiving spirit. It will destroy you and your marriage.

Remember that Jesus forgave you everything. All your debt was wiped out. Now he expects you to forgive the debts of others. Jesus told the parable of the servant whose master released him from a large debt. That servant then turned around and refused to forgive the debt of a fellow servant. His master heard of this and threw the unforgiving man to the torturers. Our refusals to forgive will also be punished.

Sometimes, when I am attacked by a desire to withhold forgiveness, I think about the second coming of

Jesus. I ask myself, "If the Lord comes this afternoon, will I be left behind because I can't forgive my husband for this?" It gives me a much better perspective on my life with Russ.

None of these things will happen overnight. There are no shortcuts to changing our attitudes and growing in respect for our husbands. We have to follow the only way that brings life and truth, Jesus himself, and follow his example of laying down his life for others day by day.

FOUR

SUBMISSION

> *Wives, submit yourselves to your husbands*
> *as to the Lord. For a husband has authority*
> *over his wife just as Christ has authority*
> *over the church; and Christ is himself the*
> *savior of the church, his body. And so wives*
> *must submit themselves completely to their*
> *husbands just as the church submits itself to*
> *Christ ... And every wife must respect her*
> *husband.*
>
> Eph. 5:22–24, 33

In a culture where authority is normally abused and exploited, it is very easy to misread Paul's letter. We probably imagine a woman who is afraid to express an opinion, who bows and scrapes abjectly before her repressive husband. He would certainly dominate her, we think; he would order her around with no regard for her needs or her dignity.

Many women have written Paul's instructions off as the ravings of a misogynist, or they simply dismiss them as a holdover from ancient Jewish culture. They might wonder why the church fathers ever accepted this as Scripture.

Properly understood, however, this passage forms the basis for a better relationship between husbands and wives. For instead of producing an intolerant, domineering husband and a scared mouse of a wife, submission in marriage can produce a concerned, loving husband and a strong supportive wife.

If you are one who pictures a submissive wife as a coward who cannot stand up for her own rights, let me ask you this: Do you think Jesus was a coward when he submitted to his Father in the crucifixion? Do you think it was a sign of weakness that he loved us so totally as to give up his life for us? No. We look at that weakness and see it as strength. It is the same with our obedience to our husbands. In our "weakness" will be our strength.

My image of a submissive wife is of a strong woman who loves the Lord with her whole being and who has willingly become a support to her husband. She has learned to speak her convictions with great love and respect, but does not try to force them upon her husband. She is secure in the love of Jesus and trusts him to sustain her. She stands proudly by her husband, letting the world see she is pleased with this man whom the Lord has made her protector.

Some women may think, "Oh, I would love to be like that. But submission would never work in my marriage. You don't know my husband."

"He doesn't act like Jesus."

"He doesn't even go to Church."

"He is already domineering."

"He refuses to make a decision."

"He doesn't believe in God."

"He opposes prayer meetings."

"He wants to argue with everything I say."

These and other circumstances may make submission very difficult. But submitting to your husband "as to the Lord" and showing him great respect is the only way that real changes in a marriage can occur. You could keep waiting for your husband to give his life to the Lord so that you can follow Scripture's teaching together. If you do, however, you will be missing out for all that time on God's plan for your life. Hopefully, your husband will someday feel as you do about Jesus. But now is the time for *you* to do what Scripture says. Now is the time to ask Jesus to change *your* heart. Now is the time to become a holy woman.

Becoming a submissive wife begins with an act of the will and a certain amount of dying to self. We must set our minds to it, then act in obedience. The difficulty of this initial decision should in itself convince us that submission to our husbands does not mean slipping into passivity. It may be one of the hardest decisions we will ever make. But if our desire is to do the will of God, we will desire to be submissive to our husbands as Scripture says we should. This will set us free to love our husband in all the ways a wife should. Our heart attitude will soon follow this act of the will.

It is helpful at a time like this to take our eyes off of ourselves and our inability to change, and to concentrate on the person of Jesus and his deep, abiding love for us. It is only in an atmosphere of total love and acceptance that we can grow and dare to change. Jesus provides that atmosphere for us. We can dare to bloom, to let him work miracles in our lives. And then we can be so filled with his Spirit of love that we can provide that love and acceptance in our homes. Jesus can do it for us. Jesus, who was submissive even to death on a cross, can teach us how to submit to our husbands.

Often a wife finds it difficult to be submissive because she fears vulnerability. According to Scripture, a husband is to love and care for his wife as Christ loves the Church. He is to be her head and protector. Unfortunately, most wives can see a great disparity between that ideal and their husbands' behavior. It is all too easy to stop right there and let resentment or bitterness build to the point where we lose even the desire to respond to the Lord by submitting to our husbands.

In my own life I have seen that although initially a husband might respond to your submission by being more domineering to test the change in you, his long-term response will be to become less repressive. If you are afraid that your husband will become more domineering if you are submissive, put your fears before the Lord and ask for the grace to trust that Jesus himself will protect and sustain you.

Or you may be afraid that your husband will refuse to make decisions you can submit to, causing a further disintegration of your marriage. Again, you have to trust the Lord to honor your desire to be submissive.

We've got to keep our eyes on Jesus. He will show us the way and give us his grace. It is true that by submitting to our husbands we become more vulnerable and open to hurt. But we also become open to great joy and deepening love. Let go of your control of your life and let the everlasting arms catch you as you fall and raise you up to new life in Jesus.

What about My Independence?

All this sounds a bit unreal in twentieth century America. The world around us tells us how wonderful and freeing total independence is. We hear that a wife can only be a full person if she has economic independence, a meaningful job, and the freedom to pursue all her own interests. Some of this sounds quite alluring, especially to a wife who is experiencing problems in her marriage.

Let me state at this point that I see absolutely nothing wrong in a wife working outside the home, pursuing a career, expanding her interests, or seeking further education. There are many good reasons for doing these things. What I object to is the propaganda for "independence." It suggests that a woman who is "only" caring for a home, offering encouragement and support to her husband, and raising her children is something less than a complete person. "Follow these roads to independence," the message seems to go, "and you will become a whole, worthwhile person."

That attitude could wear away at a woman's sense of self-worth, and cause her husband to lose his esteem for her. The truth is that Jesus died for us because in his sight we *are* special and worthwhile. He wants us to be whole persons, but only he can make us the strong, valiant women we were created to be. Only Jesus can give new meaning and purpose to our lives. He can help us to stand and not fall. Independence? Jesus is our strength. It is only as we depend on him that we are set free. And what of intellectual freedom as an end in itself? Scripture often speaks of having the mind of Christ. Which one of us wants to have "intellectual freedom" at the risk of missing the mind of Christ?

So let us be wary of wanting "independence." It can be deceptive and misleading, taking our eyes from the true source of our freedom, the Lord Jesus Christ. Jesus looks at us and says, "I am the Way, the Truth and the Life. Come to me and I will make you whole. Give your life to me and I will save it. Be utterly dependent on me and I will make you strong and utterly dependable."

I learned a valuable lesson about independence once when my husband and I were trying to find our way around a strange city. Russ was driving, but I had walked around the city earlier and had a little more familiarity with the streets. It can be nervewracking to drive in an unfamiliar city, and I could see Russ was becoming irritated. I gave my opinion about directions a few times, and once or twice Russ asked me my opinion. Each time, however, he decided on a different way. And I could see that my way would have been better.

It was a perfect situation for our tempers to flare. But then the thought struck me: what does it matter to be right? Why was it so important to me to prove that I had the better way, straighter path, superior knowledge? If Russ's failure to follow my advice meant we'd go five blocks out of our way, so what?

I relaxed after that. I still offered my suggestions but I did not care at all if they were followed. I decided to enjoy the time with my husband, and so I tried to encourage him. I even joked a little bit. The result was that we arrived at our destination feeling happy with each other and were able to enjoy our dinner. Had I spent all that time trying to prove myself right, the whole evening could have been spoiled.

This example of submission may seem like a small matter, but the principle can be applied to many situations. In fact, a wife can picture herself driving through life with her husband at the wheel. He is in charge, setting the course. Her responsibility is to support him in this. She prays that God will give her husband wisdom so that he will guide her in the right way. She submits her own ideas peacefully, resting in the protection of the Lord. If her husband makes a decision she sees as wrong, she does not fight against it, but asks Jesus to help her see how her husband views the situation. If in fact the decision does turn out wrong, she trusts that as she submits, God will show her husband the right path. She trusts Jesus, she relies on the man he has given to her, and she learns to become a humble, valiant woman.

All of this requires us to change our emphasis. Instead of concentrating on how we can change our husbands, we concentrate on how to let the Lord change *us* and leave our husbands in the hands of the Lord.

Submission and Love

I have said a lot here about submitting and serving our husbands out of obedience to Jesus. But let's not get so carried away with serving and loving for the sake of the Lord that we forget to love our husbands for their own sake. There is, and should be, a very special attraction between a husband and wife. Remember how excited we were about our husbands when we were planning our weddings? We wanted to be with them even if they were just fixing the plumbing.

That is all part of the bond that holds a couple together, that lets them enjoy touching and kissing and making love. We should let our husbands know that we enjoy that part of our marriages. The more Jesus takes over our lives, the greater will be our pleasure in our love for each other as husband and wife.

In the first letter to the Corinthians, Paul talks about many spiritual gifts—gifts of teaching, preaching, speaking in tongues, almsgiving. He speaks also of faith and hope. That is what most women want for their husbands—the fullness of the gifts, but especially faith and hope. But Paul goes on to say that without love, all the gifts are useless. Instead of wanting faith and hope so much for our husbands, let's ask for love for ourselves, for "the greatest of these is love" (1 Cor. 13:13). It is not a selfish thing to pray to become a more loving person, for that is what Jesus wants for you.

It can be very convicting to read Paul's description of love with an eye to our own marriages: "Love is patient and kind; it is not jealous or conceited or proud; love is not ill-mannered or selfish or irritable; love does not keep a record of wrongs; love is not happy with evil, but is happy with the truth. Love never gives up; and its faith, hope, and patience never fail" (1 Cor. 13:1–7).

Can we stand before God and say that we always love our husbands as we should? Do we always put the other first? Are we never irritated? Are we always ready to excuse, to trust, to hope and to endure?

I suspect that we will all answer "no." Therefore, our response to this Scripture is clear. We need to repent of everything in us that is not totally loving and accepting of our husbands. We need to ask forgiveness for all the ways we have hurt our husbands, asking it both of the Lord and of our husbands. We need to ask for an outpouring of God's grace to change our minds and hearts that we might become holy women, loving women, women who accept their husbands faults and all, just as Jesus accepted us and died for us, faults and all.

Consider this. You are privileged to have the Spirit of love dwell in your heart. The Lord supplies your needs, he comforts you, he gives you gifts you have not asked for, he speaks of his love at times when you feel irritated or unlovable. And his love dwells within you now in the power of the Spirit. "You go, then, and do the same" (Luke 10:37). Go ahead and love your husband. You will not teach him a thing by withholding your love. He will not open up a bit if you close yourself to him. Open up to your man. Love him. Woo him. Bind his wounds. Give him gifts he does not "deserve." In short, treat him as the Lord Jesus has treated you.

FIVE

ACCEPTING HEADSHIP

A woman who is baptized in the Spirit before her husband characteristically goes through several stages of growth in her spiritual life and her relationship with her husband. The first is what I have called "letting go." She realizes that she must stop urging and preaching and trying to force her husband to make a deeper commitment to the Lord. She learns to correct even those attitudes she has about his spiritual life that can be a source of pressure.

Next, she begins to grow in respect for her husband. She reads in Scripture that wives should submit to their husbands. Once she understands that submission will make her a strong, valiant woman, she makes a decision to follow Scripture's teaching. Now she is ready to put her life more fully under her husband's headship.

In the last chapter, we talked about submission mostly in terms of decisions that affect the husband and wife as a couple. But a husband's headship also extends to his wife's personal life. If he tells her to go on a diet, she should go on a diet. If he says to clean the house more thoroughly, she should improve her housecleaning. If he says to keep the house less polished, she should do that.

A wife should also submit her spiritual life to her husband. Suppose a woman attends three prayer meetings a week, goes to two Bible studies, and spends a lot of time on the phone with her Christian friends. All of these are good activities, but if it has been two days since her husband had a clean shirt, and two weeks since she has just spent some time at home with him, it would be proper for him to limit some of her "spiritual" activities.

Many women's honest reaction to this whole idea is a combination of repugnance, indignation, and anger. If a woman is trying to live a Christian life and has been given many spiritual gifts, while her husband may or may not go to church on Sunday, why should she look to him to be her spiritual head? It doesn't seem reasonable.

Let's remember, however, that the emphasis in understanding God's plan for marriage is not how well our husbands do their part, but how well we do our part. We need to pray that our husbands grow closer to the Lord, but the time to obey them is now, not when they get "holy" enough to "deserve" our obedience. If your behavior is clearly more Christian than your husband's, remember that "much is required from the person to whom much is given" (Luke 12:48). As one who has received the grace to believe, you are *expected* to live differently than someone who has not received that grace.

We should always pray that the Lord will give our husbands wisdom and discernment to guide us in our spiritual lives. We can truly rely on the Lord to bless our submission. He himself has established marriage, and he created it to function in certain ways. He has made our husbands our protectors, heads, teachers, lovers, and brothers. At times we may feel that we cannot see our husbands exercising all these functions, but we can rely on them nonetheless. The Lord brought this home to me a few years ago.

At the time, I was unable to understand why people got so excited about the second coming of Christ. I had received a good religious education; I had also been reading, going to prayer meetings, and having fellowship with other Christians. But no one could explain to me why I should be any more eager to see the Lord come in glory than to wait and see him face to face after my death. I would ask people about this, but I could never understand their answers.

Finally, I decided to ask my husband. He wasn't baptized in the Spirit then, but he was a faithful churchgoer and did have some theological background. As Russ began to answer, however, I was even more confused. So I stopped him and asked if I could pray out loud. He sighed and said, "If you keep it short." So I prayed very simply, "Lord, you have established this man as my husband and teacher. Give him the words to reach my understanding so that I may know your truth."

Russ began his explanation again, and my mind opened up. I saw the Lord's truth clearly. Others had spoken to me with as much knowledge, but the Lord was able to act in a special way through my husband.

Opening Our Lives to Our Husbands

If a husband is to guide and direct his wife in every area of her life, he obviously needs to know what is happening in every area of her life. Our lives should be an open book to our husbands. We need to tell them our ideas on subjects ranging from what color we would like the house painted to how much sleep and play the kids should get. Our husbands also need to know about our emotions—what makes us happy, what makes us angry (including specific things he does), what things hurt or sadden us.

There is a danger, however, of overwhelming our husbands with more information than they want or need to hear. The point behind opening our lives to our husbands is not to indulge in constant chatter, but to give them the information they need to make good decisions. This may take some practice.

Rather than start sharing about everything in your life all at once, I suggest taking things one at a time. When you see some way in which you or your family might need to change, take the matter to the Lord in prayer, explaining that you want your husband's direction, and then discuss it with your husband. Gradually, you will open up your whole life to him. And as he gets more used to exercising headship, your husband may even begin to bring things up to you first. Because you have been learning to accept his headship, you will be able to accept his comments more joyfully.

When we bring our ideas and emotions to our husbands, we should have an attitude of humility, not conflict. The purpose is to give them information they need to make a decision, not to manipulate them into decisions we want them to make. Let me give a couple of examples of this.

A wife turns off the television and says to her husband, "If you're going to get up on time for work tomorrow, you've got to get to bed now. I've had it with you racing around tired and out of sorts every morning." A better way to say this would be, "You're always so tired in the morning. Why don't you try going to bed an hour earlier every night for a week and see if that doesn't improve your health and disposition?"

"Some father you are! Every week for two months now you've promised to take the kids to the zoo. Why can't you keep your promise? How much effort would it take for you to spend an hour walking around with two kids?" Or, "Gee, Joe, I know you've had many things on your mind and a lot to do lately, but for the last month and a half you've been promising the kids you'd take them to the zoo. It really hurts me when I see how it frustrates the kids. They keep asking me why you won't take them."

We need to be honest, to bring all things to the light, but we need to learn to do this without putting our husbands on the defensive or telling them what to do.

After letting our husbands know what we think, we should then pray that they will make the right choice. Sometimes this will correspond with our way of thinking, and sometimes it will not. But even if it goes against our desires, we should support our husbands in their decisions. The Lord himself will honor our desire to submit to our husbands and protect us if the decision turns out to be wrong.

From Obedience to Submission

Obeying our husbands in their decisions is a good start, but we need to go one step beyond that. We need to ask for submissive hearts, too. There is a real difference between obedience and submission, although we often seem to use the words interchangeably. Obedience is an action, a type of behavior. Submission, on the other hand, is a motive, intent, or attitude of the will and heart. Let me give an example to illustrate this.

Suppose my husband decides that I am doing a more than adequate job of keeping up the house and asks me to look for a part-time job to bring in extra income. I might disagree with this decision and let him know that I disagree. If he still wants me to look for a job, I can obey him by simply applying for jobs. I can be bitter and resentful as I do this, and I would still be obeying. Or I can give this burden over to the Lord, asking him to change my heart and give me joy as I go about looking for work. That is submission. Even if we are not always joyful at first in our obedience, we can keep asking Jesus to give us the right attitude and to change our hearts. And we can believe that he will do that for us.

In fact, Jesus can take us even further. If we ask him, he will help us see the situation the way our husbands do, so that we truly become one with them in mind and heart.

Something like this happened to me once. Russ woke me up in the middle of the night to tell me that since we were tight for money I would have to look for a way to bring in $100 a week. This was to be the total after taking out taxes and the cost of a babysitter. I remember lying there with tears running down my face, silent, but screaming inside.

In my prayers about this, Jesus led me to change my heart and to trust in him. I prayed that I would have my husband's mind and heart toward the situation, and my heart actually changed.

For the next three months, I worked three part-time jobs and brought home $100 a week. Then I developed a medical problem, which put me on my back for two weeks. When I recovered, I went back to two of the jobs for a week, but was off my feet with another problem for two more weeks. After I had rested, I was able to work only one job.

Some very important things happened for Russ and me through this. He recognized that I was not fighting him; he could not accuse me of not helping out. His heart was softened as he watched my change of heart. He also saw that I was physically incapable of doing what he expected. He would not have known this if I had fought him about going to work, and he might have blamed me for not trying. At the same time, I had discovered what it was to submit in the face of a decision I thought was wrong. God clearly showed Russ that we had to proceed differently, and I learned I could trust the Lord to do that for us.

I have heard submission described as serving with joy. Let's try not to get discouraged when we see how seldom we actually do serve with joy. Jesus loves us right where we are; he will heal us and lead us to greater peace. We do not attain perfection by our own efforts, but by the grace of God. Let's put our lives in his hands and allow him to work his glory in us. Let's be like soft clay that can be molded into the shape he desires for us.

What If He Won't Take Headship?

Most of the questions asked about submission have to do with husbands who are domineering, but it is equally distressing when a wife who wants direction gets none from her husband. In America, this might be the more frequent case. A wife implores her husband to make decisions, but he either cannot or will not.

You cannot force your husband to assume headship, and it would be wrong to try to manipulate him into doing so. There are, however, some things you can do while praying for a time when your husband can give you more direction. These principles are most important for the wife of a man who will not assume headship, but they are also things every wife should do.

First, ask to be able to see yourself objectively. Jesus knows you thoroughly and wants you to be perfect. He himself will use the situations you are in to change you. So, instead of asking Jesus to change your circumstances, ask him to change you. He wants to show you where change is needed.

Next, do you respect your husband as you respect the Lord? It is very hard to respect a man who is not able to make decisions, who does not seem to protect you. But your husband's sense of self-respect can have a lot to do with his ability to give you headship. If you treat him disdainfully, you are closing the door to his self-respect and his ability to respect you.

Remember, you do not have to agree with everything your husband does in order to respect him. You just have to look at him through the eyes of one who respected him enough to die for him; who honored him enough to hang on a cross for his sake; who esteemed his life more than his own. How can you respect him when he does one thing he shouldn't or does not do another that he should? You can't, on your own. But Jesus gave up his life for your husband, knowing he would do those things. Jesus wants to give you his own love and respect for your husband.

When your husband does make a decision, support him in it. Expect it to be right. Ask the Lord to bless it. If you always show doubt about his decisions or point out later how badly they turned out, your husband will be much more unsure of himself the next time a decision is required of him.

If your husband asks you to take authority in areas where you would feel he should have headship, be peaceful and submissive. Someday, perhaps, your husband will want to be more of a leader in your home. You can pray for that day. But you cannot force him. Your place is to be faithful to what he would have you do.

This is especially true for women whose husbands are absolutely unable to take headship because of serious illness or emotional problems. If your husband is a severe alcoholic, if he suffers from mental illness or is addicted to drugs, you may have to take over completely his responsibilities in the home.

All this is very hard, but Jesus can work it in you. It would be impossible and foolish to try to live this way, were it not for the love of Jesus and his grace. He will protect you and sustain you. He will comfort you in all your hurts, for he knows that you suffer. He wants to see your husband a stronger Christian even more than you. He wants your husband to treat you as a Christian husband should more than you want it for yourself. So rest in him. He is moving powerfully in your life. He is using you to be the love of God in your home, to demonstrate the laying-down-your-life love of Jesus.

SIX

A HEART OF SERVICE

Jesus came to be your servant. Think about that for a minute. Jesus is your servant. Does that bother you, that the King of the universe came from glory to be your servant? We have gotten used to the idea that Jesus is our Savior, but it is harder to let him be our servant.

Yet Jesus wanted us to realize that this was why he came. Look at John 13:1–17:

> It was now the day before the Passover Festival. Jesus knew that the hour had come for him to leave this world and go to the Father. He had always loved those in the world who were his own, and he loved them to the very end.

Jesus knew that this was his last time with the disciples. If you were Jesus, what would you do in these last moments with your followers? Remember, this is the group you are counting on to spread your message when you are gone. Would you go over the points of the Sermon on the Mount? How about reminding them of past miracles or teaching them how to tell a good parable? Would you go over the points on being baptized and born again, or the importance of prayer?

That is not what Jesus did. Instead, he "rose from the table, took off his outer garment, and tied a towel around his waist. Then he poured some water into a washbasin and began to wash the disciples' feet and dry them with the towel around his waist . . ."

Think of the astonishment of the apostles. This was their master, a man they revered. When Jesus had finished, he sat down again and said to them, "I, your Lord and Teacher, have just washed your feet. You, then, should wash one another's feet. I have set an example for you, so that you will do just what I have done for you."

Suppose you had been with Jesus for the three years of his ministry. You had agreed with him and learned from him. You had watched the crowds listen in rapt attention, watched him do battle with corrupt leaders and perform many miracles, even raising the dead. Then one day he comes to your house and says that this is his last time to see you. You share a last meal, and afterward he says, "Let me rinse out your baby's diapers." Then he does the dishes himself, insisting that you not help. Indeed, if you do not let him do the dishes, you lose your position as his student and friend. Then, by the same time the next day, he is dead and buried. You would always remember his last two acts of service for you.

If Jesus is willing to be our servant, it follows that no one is unworthy of our service—especially our husbands. We should desire to serve them in a way that is appropriate to our role as wives.

If you have trouble figuring out the right way to serve, look at Jesus. He served as he washed the apostles' feet, and he served as he healed and ministered to all the people. He served as he prayed and as he spoke the truth to the crowds. He served as he bore persecution silently, and he served as he hung on the cross. We who follow him are called to serve in all these ways. "And he said to them all, 'If anyone wants to come with me, he must forget himself, take up his cross every day, and follow me'" (Luke 9:23).

It takes a lot of strength to take on the mind of a servant and serve brothers and sisters, husband and children. It takes a real act of the will to forget ourselves and do what another wants of us.

Jesus himself defined the attitude of a servant:

> The servant does not deserve thanks for obeying orders, does he? It is the same with you: when you have done all you have been told to do, say, "We are ordinary servants; we have only done our duty."
>
> Luke 17:9–10

This should be our attitude also. If we are keeping up the house, making it a comfortable home, working outside the home, keeping the clothes in order, preparing meals, training the children, meeting our husbands' needs, praying every day, serving the poor, keeping friendships in right relationships, "we are ordinary servants." Other translations state, "unworthy servants." So as we serve, let us have a heart full of love, doing all things for the glory of God. Only Jesus can give us new hearts—servant's hearts. Praise him whose power working in us can do more than we have ever asked or imagined.

Accepting Service

Along with giving service, we must also be ready to receive it. It has been my experience that women often fall into a trap of feeling unworthy of the service of others. We readily accept the lie that we do not deserve to have anyone taking care of us. This sometimes grows into a hardening of the heart to combat the pain of feeling so abject. You may begin to feel, "This is my house, my children, my laundry, my responsibility. I have to take care of this by myself. Nobody's going to help me and nobody should." This attitude sometimes causes women to turn down offers of help from husbands, relatives, or friends. This, in turn, can cause self-pity to show up. Many women end up with their relationships so solidly built on feelings of unworthiness or self-pity that they are caught in a dreadful web.

Jesus can cut through this web, but we have to be willing to let him do it. We have to say "yes" to becoming a new creation. We are often gripped with a fear of changing our old patterns of relating. We may not be happy the way we are, but at least we are used to it. We need to renounce that fear and give ourselves over to the love of Jesus who changes us gently, compassionately, and only for the better.

I have had firsthand experience with self-pity, the "false martyr complex," so I know how it can take hold. I remember one time when I was in college. I was feeling very discouraged—my studies were difficult, my fiance was a thousand miles away, I missed the Christian friends I had lived with during the summer, my college friends were living in distant dorms so that I seldom saw them. I went one day to the chapel to pray about my problems. In the midst of my discouragement, I sensed the Lord calling me to give up these burdens and have my heart changed.

"Oh, yes, Jesus," I said. "Take these burdens. I accept the cross you're giving me (sigh). I'll carry it (sigh), throughout the long hard year."

But I could somehow sense that the Lord didn't seem satisfied with what I was doing. I still felt him prodding me to give up my burdens. Finally I got upset and dared him.

"O.K., Lord," I said. "You know everything that's going on in my life. How do you want me to feel at this very instant?"

Immediately I was filled with such joy that I began to laugh out loud. I had to leave the chapel for fear of scandalizing the other people there.

I learned from this experience that Jesus wants us to be happy and filled with joy, even in the midst of trials.

His peace is for us, available right now for the asking.
Let's dare to be happy. Let's accept the fact that we are
worthwhile. We are, in fact, daughters of the King! As
we go through our day, let's bring that truth to mind: we
are daughters of the King, privileged to live in our Father's house, privileged to serve with joy.

We have focused quite a bit on the fact that Jesus
served and that we should serve as he did. But let's go
back to Jesus' last supper and take a look at Peter (John
13:6–9). Peter was not too happy with having Jesus wash
his feet:

> He came to Simon Peter, who said to him, "Are
> you going to wash my feet, Lord?"
> Jesus answered him, "You do not understand now
> what I am doing, but you will understand later."
> Peter declared, "Never at any time will you wash
> my feet."
> "If I do not wash your feet," Jesus answered, "you
> will no longer be my disciple."
> Simon Peter answered, "Lord, do not wash only
> my feet, then! Wash my hands and head, too!"

So Peter was not about to let Jesus serve him! And
what did Jesus reply? "If I do not wash your feet, you
will no longer be my disciple."

These words are for us, too. It's true that Jesus calls us
to serve as he serves, but it is just as true and equally
important that we allow ourselves to be served, that we
begin to let other people take care of us.

This can be terribly difficult for some women who
have prided themselves on their ability to be self-suffi-
cient. Women may even be resentful if help is offered,
considering it an insult. Yet, while it is true that we
ought to fulfill our responsibilities, it is also true that we
should be open to receiving a helping hand if it is
offered.

I know that I myself have a real urge to be a wonder woman and do all the serving in our home. Russ is usually quick to spot this tendency, however, and helps to pull me out of it. Recently, I spent a whole day baking—seven loaves of bread, muffins, a cake. In addition, I had been taking care of the children the whole time. I enjoyed the baking, but by 5:30 that day my back was beginning to hurt and my temper was growing short. Nevertheless, I began to prepare supper.

Then Russ came in, saying, "Get your coat, honey. We're going out to eat."

"Oh, no," I answered. "I can get supper."

"I know you *can* fix supper," Russ said, "but I think you need a break. Go get your coat."

I was thinking of all the reasons why we should not go out, why I should keep serving the family. But I stopped myself short and gratefully submitted to my husband's care. I came home from dinner in much better spirits, without the pain in my back or the fatigue I had felt.

Since all this might be a new experience for you, your family will probably need some suggestions as to what would be helpful. Try to be open to saying, "How about giving me a hand, here. I'm in a jam," instead of waiting for your husband or child to see your need.

Of course, many women have the opposite problem: they may be very willing to receive help, but their husbands will not give it even when the situation critically requires it. The first thing to do in such a case is to get on your knees and ask for the grace to forgive your husband. Ask God to forgive him, too. Then repent of any bitterness you have harbored against him for his lack of helpfulness. You may have to do this on several occasions.

Nagging your husband will not produce help and is wrong in itself to begin with. During a calm conversation, however, you can let your husband know that sometimes you could use his help. Then when such a time arises, you can phrase your request in a gentle, loving way, rather than nagging. For example, "Would you be able to put John's pajamas on while I get Sarah ready? I'm running behind, and we might be late for the show." This approach is much more loving than, "I don't suppose you'd want to help me get the kids ready for bed." Sometimes, however, it is right to be silent.

Some husbands might simply refuse to help. If that is the case, keep turning to the Lord for the grace of forgiveness. It is important that you allow bitterness no chance to grow.

No matter what degree of care our husbands offer us, there is one who will always be there to comfort, care for, and minister to us. Jesus wants to heal our wounds, rest our bodies, put joy in our hearts. He wants to care for us in every imaginable way. And we must let him do that for us. If we do not, we can have no part of him.

SEVEN

SUBMITTING OUR CHILDREN TO THE LORD

There are two things we should keep in mind when we talk about raising children. First, our children do not *belong* to us; they have been entrusted to us by the Lord so that we might train and love and care for them. Second, in choosing us to be parents of his children, the Lord chose both us *and* our husbands.

If your husband is not the kind of father you think he should be, pray for him. But believe deep in your heart that Jesus knows your husband through and through. He knows you and your children intimately. God did not make a mistake when he planned your family. He has a plan for your lives, and it is being worked out right in the middle of your life together.

Ideally, a husband and wife should have one mind and heart in their commitment to Jesus and in training their children. When that is not the case, the wife may experience great pain and frustration. Her husband may have very strong ideas about child-rearing that conflict with what she feels is right. Or he may have no ideas, and leave the whole responsibility for the children in her hands. Either way, she can be sorely tempted to be unsubmissive.

Whatever particular problems may be caused by the way your husband proceeds with the children, keep one central point in mind: children need to see their parents united, and they need to see biblical truths operating in their parents' lives. Your husband may not yet be living completely the way God wants, but at least you can act properly. That means being very prayerful, allowing the Spirit to make you an instrument of love toward your husband and your children.

If the children see you rebelling against your husband in the noble cause of bringing them up right, your children will learn rebellion from you. But if you demonstrate the warmth and compassion, love and submission of Jesus, the children will be attracted to Jesus. Rebellion begets rebellion, but submission begets submission. The fact that you can be counted on to have a gentle spirit and a kind word even when tempers are flying and nerves are frayed will mean more than hours of preaching. You cannot counterfeit a gentle and submissive spirit. You have to let Jesus work it in you.

In other words, the most important gift we have to offer our children and the most effective thing we can do to train them is to be in a right relationship with our husbands. Practically speaking, this means giving up our own ways of doing things in order to support our husbands. If your husband believes in giving a lot of spankings, you spank a lot. If he believes in no spankings, then you do not spank. Of course, you should tell your husband your own ideas and concerns in the matter. But remember that he does have ears. You do not have to keep repeating something for him to hear you. It is enough to simply let him know how you feel. Should he then decide to proceed in another way, support him in that decision.

For example, your husband might decide that the children should never be spanked. If you, seeing the children are becoming undisciplined, take it upon yourself to spank them, what have you gained? The children will know that you are not backed up by their father, so they will respond only half-heartedly. Your husband will never see the effect of having no discipline, and so he may never change his mind. You lose out all around by taking matters into your own hands.

Nurturing

There are some ways to nurture our families without taking over or fighting our husbands' authority. They may not seem very dramatic or powerful, but God can use them to melt the hearts of our families.

First, we need to be faithful to church attendance, even though our husbands might not go with us. We do not need to make a big show of this; we can even get up before the rest of the house to go to an early service. Some women are unable to go to church regularly because it upsets their husbands; in these cases, the wife should talk to her pastor and see what can be worked out. But women who are in a position to go to church should go, taking the children if their husbands will allow it.

If we can possibly meet with other Christian women for fellowship, we should do that. We need support from others. But we should also make sure that our conversation at home consists of more than our explicitly Christian activities and meetings, otherwise we will turn off our families quickly. A few sentences about how a meeting went or some happy news from it is usually as much as the family will want to hear, unless they become genuinely interested in hearing more.

Attending a local prayer meeting can be helpful, but we must be careful not to put prayer group activities above the welfare of our families. Our first place is with them, nurturing and loving them. Christian meetings are important because they help form us into women who can bring the love of God into our homes, but they will have the opposite effect if most of our energy goes there instead of to our families.

Keeping our houses in order and preparing food with love are good ways to nurture our families and bring love into their lives. It is important to spend time with our children—both time alone with each child and time in activities with all the children. If you cannot think of ways to go about this, ask the Spirit to enlighten you and ask other women how they do it. We should also take time alone with our husbands if they would like that. If your husband is seldom at home, make sure that home becomes the most inviting place he goes.

Speaking gently about the love of God is another way to bring his love into our homes. But we need to be wary of our motives. It is not loving to hit people over the head with the love of God, or to use it to evoke guilt. Most women do well to *be* the word of God for their family rather than to *speak* it.

We should do what we can to teach our children about the Lord. Bedtime is a natural time to teach them night prayers. But it is not the wife's role to initiate a regular family prayer time or Bible study unless her husband has explicitly asked her to do this. The children need to know their mother has their father's authority behind her.

We can offer prayers for healing as we bandage sores and kiss scraped knees. My children usually smile in spite of themselves when they come in with a bruise and I remind them, "There's medicine in these lips! Let me kiss you." But they also expect Jesus to do the healing and will often ask for prayers. Older children's hurts— a harsh word, a low mark on a test, rejection and loneliness—are harder to kiss away. But children should know that we are behind them, loving them and supporting them, and that we are taking their needs to the Father in intercession.

Prayer, then, is a final way we can nurture our families. We should pray always. Instead of talking to ourselves as we mop the floor, we can talk with Jesus. When we pray, we should bring the needs of our families before the Lord. We pray for our husbands, that they will be directed by God. We pray for ourselves, that we may become the women God wants us to be. And we pray for our children, that they grow up in the knowledge and love of God, even if we must wait many years to see them accept him fully.

Sometimes, the greatest heartaches of raising children are caused by holding on to them too tightly. Just as we have to let go of our husbands so that the Lord himself can touch them, so we must let go of our children. We must teach and train them, but we cannot force children to change their minds and hearts. We can correct their behavior and instruct them in the mind of Christ, but only God can mold their hearts. If we see our children as extensions of ourselves or if we try to live our life over through theirs, we will be in for frustration and disappointment.

One of the great figures of Christian history, St. Augustine, was thirty years old before he gave his life to Christ. His mother, Monica, is also considered a saint, primarily because she prayed for Augustine throughout those thirty years. She never despaired that he would accept the salvation that Jesus offers to us all. This should also be our mark as Christian mothers.

We have taken a good look at our responsibilities as wives in terms of loving our husbands and children. But how do we get personally equipped to be this type of woman—strong, loving, respectful, supportive? In the next two chapters, I want to take a look at some of the supports we need for ourselves, especially our relationship with the Lord and our fellowship with other Christian women.

EIGHT

A FOUNDATION OF PRAYER

We do not become strong, holy women purely by our own efforts. Many times we will face burdens that are too heavy for us, or have to make changes that seem impossible, or run into insurmountable problems. If we try to struggle through these situations on our own, we will fail. We must rely on God's help. That is why I have emphasized so many times in this book: "You can't do this yourself. Turn to Jesus. Ask the Holy Spirit for help. Go to your Father."

If you want to begin living in the way I am suggesting in this book, the most practical help I can give is to emphasize prayer. Regular prayer is not simply helpful; it is crucial. An attempt to live a married life on scriptural principles without a foundation of prayer would be absurd, frustrating, and doomed to failure.

Because we do need God's help, it is important that we develop a relationship in which we naturally turn to him and experience his strength. A close, loving relationship with the Lord develops in much the same way as a loving relationship between two people—through regular contact and communication.

When a man and woman are in love, they spend lots of time with each other. They have serious talks, make plans, go out to have fun, sit quietly together. They learn each other's ways, each other's thoughts, each other's likes and dislikes.

When the two marry, they discover even more about each other. In order to become one, they must each die to self, sacrifice, forgive, keep loving. What a beautiful sight to see an older couple who are in harmony with each other. Looking at them, one cannot help but think of the many joys and sufferings they have come through together, forging them into a living symbol of unity.

The same principles apply to our relationship with God. Jesus has taken the first steps toward us. He knows our ways and our mind, and has chosen to love us. He invites us to get to know him better through prayer, to learn his ways and put on his mind. He asks us to share all our lives with him. These are the preliminaries to a more solid relationship, to real unity with the Lord. These preliminaries are critical. They are the foundational lines of communication with God that we will use throughout our lives.

It is helpful, even crucial, to see prayer in terms of a relationship with the Lord. Prayer is not a formality. It is a conversation with the person who loves us more than any other ever could. Because prayer is so central to the growth of our relationship with Jesus, I am including here some basic suggestions for how to develop a deeper prayer life.

First of all, we need to *commit ourselves to daily prayer*. We need regular contact with the Lord to develop a good, loving relationship with him. We can ask Jesus to help us be faithful to this commitment.

Next, we can ask the Lord for the *ability to pray*. Many people feel that they cannot pray—that they do not know how or what to do. If this is a problem, we can ask God to teach us how to pray, how to open up to him, how to receive his love and his word. This is a gift he wants us to have. Remember, "everyone who asks will receive, and anyone who seeks will find, and the door will be opened to him who knocks" (Matt. 7:8).

Our *interior attitudes*, especially a spirit of humility and forgiveness, are important to our prayer. We cannot expect to develop a close relationship with the Lord if we refuse to let go of resentment against another person. Jesus tells us, "So if you are about to offer your gift to God at the altar, and there you remember that your brother has something against you, leave your gift there in front of the altar, go at once and make peace with your brother, and then come back and offer your gift to God" (Matt. 5:23–24).

It is important that the time we have for prayer be *free of distractions.* To find a time that will not be interrupted, we may need to get up earlier, go to bed later, or plan around the children's schedule. We should experiment with our time, and then, when we find a good time for prayer, stick with it. For distractions that do come to mind when we are praying—suddenly remembering an important message, for example—it is helpful to keep a notebook and pen handy. We can jot down anything that we will need to remember later, then turn our minds back to the Lord.

We should also *relax* when we pray. Some people are afraid to draw close to the Lord because they think he will stop loving them if he finds out what they are really like. But Jesus already knows us thoroughly—even our hidden faults—and loves us anyway. He died to tell us that he loves the unlovable, that he can forgive the unforgivable. If we have problems with any sin or temptation, we can tell him. He knows our struggles and will help us deal with them.

Besides being relaxed in spirit, I often find it helpful to relax physically before I pray. I get in a comfortable position, usually sitting. (Lying down is also comfortable, but usually puts me to sleep.) I unfold my arms and uncross my legs, because I find that folded arms and crossed legs can signal defenses I have unconsciously placed between myself and the Lord. I shake my arms limply like a rag doll to relax them. And I smile, praising God with my mouth even though I may not feel like doing so.

The amount of *time* each person should spend in prayer varies. A long-distance runner does not start out doing ten miles a day. He builds up by practice and perseverence. In the same way, our prayer life develops gradually through our faithfulness and perseverence. Under the guidance of the Holy Spirit, our communication with the Lord will become more free, and we may want to spend increasingly longer times in prayer. At the beginning, however, ten or fifteen minutes a day, free from distraction, is a good amount of time for prayer. Even if we do not at first actually pray during that whole time, it gives us the freedom to wait on the Lord. Later, we may find that even an hour spent in prayer seems short.

Finally, we must *endure.* Sometimes prayer is a joy; sometimes our prayer time seems dry and distracted. Either way, we need to keep on praying. Our prayer may be dry because God has begun to speak to us in a new way, and we have not yet caught on to him. It may be dry because we have not repented of some disobedience. Sometimes it is because we lack forgiveness; sometimes our prayer is dry for no discernible reason at all. No matter what their cause, we must ask for the grace to remain faithful to daily prayer during times of dryness. Jesus longs to be with us and rejoices when we turn to him. He will always honor our prayer, even though we may not always feel his presence.

The Lord's Prayer

Jesus taught us to pray by giving us a prayer. Let's take a brief look at the Lord's Prayer. If we understand its main points, it can be a help in our prayer times.

Our Father: When we call on God, we are calling on our loving Father. This does not mean that we do not also pray to Jesus or to the Holy Spirit. To give honor to one is to honor all three persons of the Trinity, for they are one God.

who art in heaven: This reminds us of the reverence we owe God. He is our Father, but he is also the holy Lord of the heavens. We stand in the presence of the Almighty.

hallowed be thy name: The Good News Bible reads, "May your holy name be honored" (Matt. 6:9). The first element of our prayer time, then, is to put ourselves in the Lord's presence, remembering the relationship he has established with us, and to worship him. We can worship in confidence and trust, because we have already been reminded that God loves us as his children.

Thy kingdom come, thy will be done, on earth as it is in heaven: We pray in expectation of God's reign. We are hopeful. And we submit our own wills, asking that they come perfectly into accord with God's will. Think what the world would be like if God's will was done on earth as it is in heaven. Think what our lives would be like if we personally did only God's will instead of wasting time with our own plans.

Give us this day our daily bread: In the gospel of Matthew (6:8), Jesus says, "Your Father already knows what you need before you ask him." Yet he includes this petition in his prayer. Even though God knows our needs, it is right that we ask him for his help. In this way, we are reminded of our dependence on God instead of thinking things are going well because of our own brilliance. When we do ask the Lord, let's also thank him and believe our prayer has already been answered.

and forgive us our trespasses, AS WE FORGIVE THOSE WHO TRESPASS AGAINST US: I added the emphasis here because Jesus himself emphasized this point. "If you forgive others the wrongs they have done to you, your Father in heaven will also forgive you. But if you do not forgive others, then your Father will not forgive the wrongs you have done" (Matt. 6:14). This must have struck Jesus' listeners very forcibly. It should strike us, too. If we do not forgive, our own failings will not be forgiven. Let's pray, then, for a forgiving heart. Let's not keep ourselves miserable and unhappy, and let's not do that to others.

And lead us not into temptation, but deliver us from evil: The Good News Bible translates this, "Do not bring us to hard testing, but keep us safe from the Evil One" (Matt. 6:13). We ask protection from our enemy, the devil. Jesus is victorious over evil, and we rely on his power in our own struggles with the enemy. We know the power of the cross and resurrection.

For thine is the kingdom and the power and the glory, forever. Amen. We can use the Lord's Prayer as a guide for our prayer. We begin by putting ourselves in God's presence, worshipping and praising him. We submit our wills to his, and put on the mind of Christ. We ask him to supply our needs and the needs of others we know. We listen for his word. We may sing, read psalms, pray for a passage. If we have a favorite devotional book, that can also become part of our prayer time. We should let the Spirit move freely in our prayer.

Listening to the Lord

When I talk with other women about prayer, I am often asked, "What do you mean by 'hearing the Lord speak to me'?" Or, "How can I be sure that it is the Lord I hear in prayer and not just some idea of my own—even the voice of Satan?" Prayer can be very frustrating when we do not understand how to listen to God's voice. Yet the actual experience of "hearing the Lord" is very simple and natural.

One important step in learning to hear the Lord is to give him a chance to speak. Sometimes, we go to pray with our mind so full of our own problems that we do all the talking without listening for a response. It is a good idea to spend some time being quiet before the Lord, waiting for any word he might have.

When the Lord does speak, his word rarely takes the form of a shattering voice from the clouds. We may simply have a sense that a particular idea or direction is his will for us. Or we may find words and thoughts coming spontaneously to mind. We may feel drawn to a particular passage of Scripture, or sense that the Lord is speaking in something a friend says or in something we have read. The Lord's voice can come in many ways, and often the only way we recognize it is by an inner conviction that this thought or Scripture or comment has been directed to us by God.

How can we be sure, though? After all, the word we hear may get mixed up with our own ideas, or with our selfishness and pride. Inner promptings can even come from Satan, who wants to confuse and mislead us. Although I grant that there is some danger of being misled when we try to hear the Lord, I do not think we need to worry a lot about it. For the Lord has given us some simple tests that will always keep us on the right path.

One is the peace of Christ. If we receive some word or sense that frightens or upsets us, we should suspect that it is not the Lord speaking. God's word is a word of love—even when he is convicting us of sin—and brings peace with it.

Another test is Scripture. The Lord never contradicts his own revelation, so if what we hear disagrees with Scripture, we know it is not from God. If we are uncertain about something that seems to be a word from the Lord, we should ask him to guide us to a Scripture passage that will confirm what he is saying.

A third safeguard is the discernment of other Christians. As long as we are willing to submit to the judgment of our brothers and sisters and of our churches, we will be protected from real error. We can also trust that the Lord himself will protect us as long as we are trying to be faithful to him and are making our best effort to discern his word. The closer we grow to Jesus, the better will we be able to recognize his voice.

Pray in the Spirit

The final thing I want to say about prayer is that even in this we are not left to our own resources. The Spirit will pray through us. Scripture says, "For we do not know how we ought to pray; the Spirit himself pleads with God for us in groans that words cannot express. And God, who sees into our hearts, knows what the thought of the Spirit is" (Rom. 8:26–27).

Let's ask the Lord to help us yield to him, to help us let go of our own efforts to pray and ask the Spirit to take over. If we give our minds to God, he will be free to fill them with himself. If we give over our spirits to God, he will be free to fill them also. Let's give over our bodies to God, too, for the praise and worship of his name. We can sit, kneel, stand, dance, jump, raise our hands, clap, and bow as the Spirit leads us. Not that we will do all these things in every prayer time, but let's not put limits on how God wants to work.

NINE

DAUGHTERS OF THE KING

You are a daughter of the King. Jesus wants you to know and believe that in your inmost heart. We are all daughters of the King, privileged to dwell in the courts of the Lord of Heaven. "Enter the Temple gates with thanksgiving; go into its courts with praise. Give thanks to him and praise him" (Ps. 100:4). Since our marriages do not exist in a social vacuum, it is important to learn about our relationships with other Christian women—our sisters in the courts of the Lord. Sometimes, these relationships can have great influence on us as women and as wives.

Our King is a very special kind of king. He is just and merciful, holy, glorious, and above every other. It only follows that those who dwell in his courts should behave differently than those who have frequented the courts of earthly kings.

Throughout much of human history, courtiers have been known for their gossip, slander, intrigue, licentiousness, manipulation, office seeking, and love of pleasure and finery. The courts of the Lord are very different. Paul often speaks of how to behave in his courts:

> So get rid of your old self, which made you live as you used to . . . and put on the new self, which is created in God's likeness . . .
>
> Eph. 4:22–24

Let love make you serve one another ...

Gal. 5:13

My brothers, if someone is caught in any kind of wrongdoing, those of you who are spiritual should set him right; but you must do it in a gentle way ... Help carry one another's burdens, and in this way you will obey the law of Christ.

Gal. 6:1–2

We are daughters of the King. We have many sisters who are also daughters of the King. Jesus wants to renew our minds and hearts and teach us new ways to relate to these sisters in Christian fellowship. It is hard to live without fellowship, yet it seems rare to find women having a good, fruitful relationship with other women.

A few years ago many women in my community were feeling very isolated even though they had many brothers and sisters. We saw each other frequently at prayer meetings or showers or other activities, and we were quite affectionate in our hugs and greetings. Yet we had no regular opportunity to share our lives in depth.

As we became aware of this problem, some women agreed to spend a certain amount of time together each week for fellowship. Two things soon became apparent. First, many women had experienced such unfortunate relationships with other women in the past that they were reluctant to get together with women at all. Second, even those who wanted fellowship did not know quite how to go about it.

We have learned a lot about fellowship in the years since, and have come to depend on these groups as a vital part of our community. I would like to share with you some of the truths that have helped us to grow to this point, because I believe that fellowship is especially important for women who are involved in the charismatic renewal without their husbands. You need support and encouragement that can be found in friendship with other women. A wife who lacks fellowship tends to put enormous pressure on her husband because he must fulfill *all* her needs. Since one person obviously is not equipped to do that, she can become frustrated, resentful and bitter.

Starting a Fellowship Group

You may be able to get a good deal of fellowship through informal contact with your friends, but most women find it helpful to have regular, reliable contact with a stable group. There are several ways to start a fellowship group. A prayer group may decide to organize smaller sharing groups for its members, a weekly Bible study can provide fellowship, or a group of women can just decide on their own to get together regularly. Whatever type of group you have, I would like to suggest some ideas that can help things run more smoothly.

First, the women in the group should agree to meet together regularly. Many groups try to meet once a week, but the exact schedule is not so important as agreeing to come to the meetings faithfully.

It is usually good to have someone act as leader of the group. She can call everyone to honor the group's agreements, and she can help keep the group's discussions on track. She should be a woman strong in faith, but not domineering.

It is also good to agree that the group will have only one conversation at a time. We might miss the very thing Jesus wanted us to hear if we are in the middle of another conversation when it is said. Besides, it is polite and respectful to listen to the person who is speaking.

Finally, we should avoid letting the conversation in a group center on our personal problems. Most of us have our share of problems, and our sisters in the fellowship groups can sometimes help us learn how to deal with them. Too much emphasis on our problems, however, can begin to wear us down instead of building us up. We need to remember that the purpose of our groups is not to get all our problems worked out, but to find fellowship and encouragement among other Christian women.

One real danger when a women's group focuses on problems is that it slips into giving a type of personal direction that is not appropriate. A fellowship group is not supposed to provide pastoral direction for its members; our primary direction should come from our husbands. I know, however, that for many years pastoring was the only way I related to other women—either I was giving them advice, or they were giving me advice. I do not think that I ever seriously intended to take anyone's advice, although I did on occasion; this type of relationship was mainly a way I could keep myself safe and at arm's length from my friends. One or the other of us was always higher or lower; we never related purely as equals.

If you find your group slipping into this pattern, try taking a break for a couple of weeks. Go out to lunch together, go to the park, clean somebody's attic. We need more to our relationship as sisters than problem-solving. We need to become friends. Swap recipes, cut out a dress, make curtains, hang wallpaper—there is a lot we can do together. Our relationships as women should not be limited to doing things together, of course, but these activities are a helpful way to vary a group's meetings.

There is really no blueprint that every group should follow. Each group is as unique as its members. None will proceed in quite the same way. Some might do better with a heavy emphasis on Scripture study. Others might study worthwhile books. Some might all bring handiwork, and some might just sit and talk. Whatever your group does, just remember that Jesus is the head of it, prayer should be a part of it, and love should be the core of it. Be willing to make a few mistakes as you learn the right ways to share your lives together.

And be patient with each other. I remember the first women's fellowship group I was in. I was living in Wareham, Massachusetts, and the Lord led me to a group of Spirit-filled women the first week I arrived. I talked a lot about many things in that group, but I'll bet it was four months before anyone even knew how big my family was. I praise God that those sisters cared so much for me that they were patient and warm, and that they loved me as I began to open up parts of my life I thought they would despise me for.

The women I know have learned many valuable lessons about how to carry on fellowship in a manner befitting the courts of the Lord. In the rest of this chapter, I want to discuss some principles for our conduct and speech with other women.

Building Trust

One important principle for any kind of fellowship group is that the women in it must be able to trust one another. The Lord wants us to believe that what our sister tells us is true, without trying to judge her motives. I think this more than anything else has helped me learn to trust others. If you have a women's fellowship group, I suggest that you agree to take one another at her word and not try to judge each other's motives. Be very explicit about this agreement until you have it worked into your hearts. Keep bringing it up in conversation and taking it before the Lord in prayer. It may seem obvious that people should relate on the basis of trust, but I have found that it is very hard to take another person at her word while assuming that she is speaking from the best possible motive.

Suppose a friend tells me a week before a party that she is quite sure that everyone is coming in casual attire. Then, on the night of the party, I find that I am the only person who has come in casual clothes. Everyone else is quite dressed up, including my friend. She comes over to me to say, very apologetically, that she had tried to call me about five times to tell me of the change, but then got so busy that she forgot. If I take her at her word, I can accept her apology, forgive her, then either stay at the party in my casual clothes or go home to change.

However, if I am not standing firm on these truths, I might start wondering if she ever really tried to call me, or if she even wanted to. Maybe I am such a nobody that she never even thought of me. Or maybe I offended her somehow and she was trying to get back at me by causing embarrassment. Maybe the hostess was in on it, too.

This gives some indication of how damaging it can be to doubt a person's word or assume that her motives are not good. It makes for poor relationships, breeds fear and mistrust, and can eventually end a friendship.

Negative Humor

What is negative humor? It's saying what you don't mean in a joking way. It's sarcasm. It's a happy put-down.

Why is it so hard on relationships? Because someone must always be the butt of the joke. Negative humor often plays on a real quality of the person and almost always leaves the doubt, "Did she really mean that and was afraid to say it to my face?"

If you joke that my clothes are so pretty I must be trying to attract all the men, I begin to wonder if something about my clothes and behavior is actually wrong.

If you joke about how much I serve my husband, I might lose some of my desire to serve him.

If I am singing hymns around my house and you ask if I am practicing up for the Mormon Choir, I might think twice about singing hymns around the house again.

The hard part about giving up negative humor is that it is often ingrained in us. It's safe, and it's humorous. We need humor in our lives, but not at the expense of hurting a brother or sister.

The substitute for negative humor is Paul's instruction: "Encourage one another and help one another" (1 Thess. 5:11). Learn to encourage one another and be encouraged in love. Tell your sisters about the changes you can see Jesus bringing about in them. Tell them how much you admire their taste in clothes, tell them how pleased you were for a kindness shown your child. And feel free yourself to bask in the warmth of being told how you have been obeying Jesus. We have a lot to talk about, believe it or not.

Gossip

Remember that I mentioned gossip as something found in earthly courts, but not in the courts of the King? Unfortunately, it seems to be one of the hardest habits for women to put away when they enter the courts of the Lord. Often we develop a blind spot to what we are doing and end up "gossiping in the Lord." It is still gossip because it reveals information that either we have no business relaying or our hearers have no need or right to hear. It appears, however, to be "in the Lord" because we pass this information on in a tone of real concern or as a prayer of petition. It can sound something like this:

"Please pray with me for my neighbor, Jane Doe, who has been a secret alcoholic for years. There's been a lot of fighting over at their house lately, and last night I saw her husband leave with two suitcases." A simple, "My neighbors could use our prayers this morning for a special touch of the Lord's love," would be sufficient.

I am always grateful for the gift of tongues when praying for needs. The Spirit will pray through us and he knows the needs of others much better than we do.

Another subtle way to gossip is to ask, "How is Ruth doing? I haven't seen her at a prayer meeting for such a long time." If you are truly concerned, don't ask about her. Give her a call or go to visit.

Pegging two young people as a likely couple for marriage seems innocent enough, but it is a form of gossip that can hinder their relationship. Two people who are going together have enough pressures without the force of our opinions on what they should do. It is important that we not interfere with what the Lord may be doing with them. When a couple's engagement *should* be made public knowledge, they will announce it. We should wait patiently for that time without giving in to that desire to be able to say, "I told you two years ago that was a match!"

Personal testimony can also become a form of gossip. We need to be very prudent when discussing the testimony of another person, and we have to be careful when giving our own. If we spend ten minutes of our testimony talking about all our past sins and four seconds saying, "But Jesus saved me from that," we will impress our hearers mostly with how much Satan was able to work in our life. Sordid details of our personal testimony can usually be omitted, and the time spent in showing how Jesus cared for us even in the midst of darkness.

If this is true of our own testimony, it is even more true when we discuss another's testimony. We do not have the right to use a person's testimony to shock or impress others. Most personal testimony is best left to the person whose testimony it is.

Remember, "the mouth speaks what the heart is full of" (Matt. 12:34). If you have a problem curbing your tongue, spend more time in prayer, read Scripture more, cultivate a heart of love, and set your mind on good, useful, and holy matters. Then when you speak you will be full of good things to share. The letter of James offers very good advice on the use of the tongue.

You can also ask the Lord to set a guard on your tongue, so that you will not say what you shouldn't.

Speaking the Truth in Love

Conversation in any group may sometimes turn in the wrong direction—toward gossip, or negative humor, or criticism of another person. When someone recognizes this, she should point out the problem to the group or to the person speaking. The leader has a special responsibility for this, but every woman in the group should be free to offer a correction when one is necessary.

Before you speak to correct, however, be sure there is some wrongdoing involved. For example, if the leader knows that a conversation has taken a damaging turn, she needs to speak in love to correct the problem. If you really love your sister, you will want to help her to be more holy. If you really love the other sisters in the group, you will want to steer them away from damaging sharings. Although occasionally things need to be dealt with right away to protect the group, you should approach your sister privately whenever possible. We do not want to stifle a sister or make her feel badly about herself. We do not want to make her afraid of saying anything for three months, nor do we want her never to come back. Private talks of correction should be face to face, not over the phone.

Before you correct a sister be sure to tell her, "I love you," and be able to mean it. Otherwise do not even open your mouth. You will do more harm than good.

Do not be afraid to say that you feel terrible about correcting someone. It will make you more human and prevent you from sounding cold and unfeeling. Say that it is hard, speak of your love, and state the truth simply. Hug each other. Talk about it in the group if that seems right. We all need to learn from each other's mistakes.

Although it might be nice if everyone met correction with gratitude, that is not usually the case. Correction is hard for most of us to take, and nothing we say can make any impact unless the Spirit himself does the convicting. So leave the convicting to God. Do not expect total agreement or open reception to a correction. We are all growing toward that, but one often needs private time for the words to sink in. Be open yourself to correction by other members of the group, including correction on how to correct.

Sharing about Husbands

I would like to share at some length about how to talk with other women about our relationships with our husbands, especially when we are experiencing difficulty. We need to help each other with this. I cannot set up rules to encompass every situation, but there are some guidelines and examples that might be of help.

The first thing to keep in mind is to honor your husband. You may be so angry or hurt some days that you would like to tell the whole world how badly he treated you, but don't do it. Forgive him and take your hurt to the Lord. At the same time, you can talk about some things in a way that will allow other women to share their wisdom with you without dishonoring your husband.

A few weeks ago, one woman in my fellowship group shared how she had really blown it during the week: she had ordered her husband to stop watching so much T.V. and get into bed. Another said she had turned off the T.V. and told her husband to go to bed. There are seven in our group, and we all began to laugh as each woman shared how she had tried to boss her husband away from the T.V. and into bed. We couldn't believe we had done this when we all thought we were so submissive. When we recovered from our laughter, one of the women remarked that even though we had shared about our lack of submission in that matter, at least we shared it submissively. Not one of us had said that her *husband* had a problem. We knew that the problem to deal with was our own.

But sometimes husbands do have problems that we need help in understanding or dealing with.

My husband has long had trouble getting up in the morning. He has had up to three alarm clocks going off simultaneously in different parts of the room. He has had juice given him, breakfast and work awaiting him, and still the problem has remained. This used to leave me tied up in knots. If Russ got up late, he was not in a very good mood. Somehow I managed to assume the blame and guilt for all of this.

While we were living in Massachusetts, I shared this with the women I fellowshipped with. One woman had had the same problem, and spoke some very liberating words to me. She said that I could not force Russ out of bed. I should do what I could to get him up on time, but the decision was his. I should not assume any guilt for his failure to get up unless I was contributing to it by lying in bed myself after the alarms went off—which Russ had expressly asked me not to do. The women also offered a couple of suggestions for helping to get him up.

This was an appropriate problem to share with my fellowship group. It would have been wrong, however, if I had given a blow-by-blow description of a morning when Russ was particularly out of sorts. No one but Jesus has a right to know what my husband said in anger. And even Jesus does not want to hear me complaining. He will listen to me crying out in pain and rage, "Help me. I'm so angry I could kill him!" He will bring peace and comfort to my soul. But I cannot sit there, coldly telling Jesus every harsh thing my husband said in a spirit of "Go get him for that, Lord." Jesus wants to help me with my emotions. He does not want me to keep dwelling bitterly on my husband's faults, real or imagined.

It is important to honor your husband, even if it means not sharing a problem until a time when you are sufficiently calm to do so properly. One good way to share might be, "I'm not sure whether I should go to both meetings a week or not. Joe hasn't said one way or another, so I just don't know." With that as an opener, the other women in the group may be able to find out how you posed the question to Joe, whether your question was well timed (was he in the middle of his shower?), whether you were direct, whether he responded indirectly. They may advise you to ask him again, or tell you to offer to stay home for a couple of weeks. There are ways to get help with questions or problems without dishonoring our husbands.

The Difference Between Dumping and Sharing Negative Things

One question that often comes up in a fellowship group is how to share about things that are troubling us without becoming negative or criticizing other people. Again, I cannot give answers here to fit every situation, but there are some fundamental rules that can help us.

Dumping occurs when you speak out of bitterness, disappointment, anger, resentfulness, hurt, or frustration, without any concern for what the Lord would have you say or for the people you are talking about. When you are in the process of "dumping," you usually are not looking for a solution, a word of wisdom or love. All you want is to let your hearer know how rotten things are and how rotten you feel.

Dumping does not help you feel better. It will either leave you feeling guilty, or will make your situation seem worse than it was before. Discontent breeds discontent. "Guard against turning back from the grace of God. Let no one become like a bitter plant that grows up and causes many troubles with its poison" (Heb. 12:15).

What do you do, then, when life seems overwhelming? When everything seems to be crashing down around you? When you are filled with rage or hurt?

First, you should run to the Lord. If you think of running anywhere or everywhere else first, it probably means you want to share your burden out of a wrong motive. So run to the Lord, cry out to him in your distress, bang your pillow, sob, yell—whatever it takes, but do it working toward the goal of letting Jesus give you his mind and heart for the situation. Cry out, "Father, I am in such pain. Help me. Give me your mind. Give me your heart. Let me be in the center of your will."

Even then, however, you may still feel some bitterness or frustration or confusion. How do you share these things with your sisters?

The first thing to do is to ask them to pray with and for you. Tell them that you are feeling terribly burdened, that you do not want to dishonor anyone, and ask for prayer that you share in a right way. Occasionally that may be all you can say: you will not be able to share any particulars because of the other people involved. In that case, the group should respond by being open to prophecy or Scripture for you. Just hugging you and telling you they love you is a help.

Most of the time, however, you can share at least enough particulars to give some idea of what is troubling you. And certainly you should share your own troublesome emotions—the bitterness, anger, or depression you feel. Other women, who may have dealt successfully with these problems, can give you valuable suggestions.

When you do share some particulars about a given situation, it should be with a firm intention to dishonor no one. Your aim should be to find out how you can act to help the situation. There are no clear guidelines here as to what exactly you should share. But if you have gone first to the Lord, have asked for prayer from your group, and are ready to stop talking if people in the group feel you are out of line, then you should trust the Lord and go ahead with what seems right. You may make some mistakes, but that is often a way to grow.

We should not share a problem with our group when we know that we ought to be going directly to the person involved for reconciliation. The time to share a problem is when we need insight and wisdom and sound advice from others. Our sisters may be able to put our problems in perspective. They can also help out, depending on the nature of the problems. Perhaps you need help knowing how to clean house, or need time away from the children, or your washer is broken. In all things, we can build each other up in love.

If a woman has greater needs than the group can or should handle, she should find someone in a position to offer more pastoral help. Perhaps her pastor or his wife, her priest, or a more mature Christian woman. But be careful not to go advice hopping. Even wise pastors can have different approaches to problems. If you keep picking and choosing the advice you want, you are not going to get the help you need.

There is a great deal we all must learn in order to have good fellowship. We can trust Jesus to guide us and be with us as we learn to dwell in his courts. We are growing into the women God wants us to be. We do not have to fear each other any longer. We do not have to be isolated from each other. Paul offers us a good picture of who we are becoming.

Remind your people to submit to rulers and authorities, to obey them, and to be ready to do good in every way. Tell them not to speak evil of anyone, but to be peaceful and friendly, and always to show a gentle attitude toward everyone.

Titus 3:1–2

In the same way instruct the older women to behave as women should who live a holy life. They must not

be slanderers or slaves to wine. They must teach
what is good, in order to train the younger women to
love their husbands and children, to be self-con-
trolled and pure, and to be good housewives who
submit themselves to their husbands, so that no one
will speak evil of the message that comes from God.

Titus 2:2–5

"So that no one will speak evil of the message that
comes from God." That the courts of the King may
reflect the glory of the Lord.

So—we are daughters of the King, living in his glorious courts. How privileged we are to discover how to
dwell as sisters there. How tenderly we should view
each other, all equally precious in the King's eyes. Let's
approach our task with joy and humility. We are not yet
perfect, so let's not expect perfection. But we can expect to learn together, to laugh, cry, hug, forgive, grow,
share, and be forgiven. What a glorious lot has been
given to us. What a glorious King we serve!

TEN

REMAINING PEACEFUL AS OUR HUSBANDS CHANGE

*In the same way you wives must submit
yourselves to your husbands, so that if any
of them do not believe God's word, your
conduct will win them over to believe. It
will not be necessary for you to say a word,
because they will see how pure and reverent
your conduct is.*

1 Peter 3:1-2

This is the only passage in Scripture directed specifi-
cally to the wife of a non-Christian husband. It also
says much to the wife whose husband is Christian, but
does not share her degree of commitment to the Lord.
I have waited until now to introduce this passage because it focuses on winning over our husbands to Jesus,
which is not our *primary* goal in becoming holy women.
But now that we have a fuller picture of how a wife
should relate to her husband, this is a good Scripture to
turn to.

We *should* want our husbands to be holy, for that is
what God wants. God created our husbands to give him
glory, to love and serve him. And we should want our
husbands to know the Lord more personally so that they
may experience the peace and joy we have come to
know. Often, however, the real reason we want our
husbands to come closer to the Lord is that we think it
will make our own lives easier. We look forward to the

day our husbands are baptized in the Spirit as a day when our lives—not theirs—will finally be right.

Commonly, all three of these attitudes are intermingled in our minds. But as we accept the teachings of the Lord and live as he wants, he can work to purify our attitudes. We learn to accept the fact that while our husbands' relationships with Jesus may not be all that they should, these men are still our heads. We learn to concentrate on becoming holy women ourselves, leaving our husbands' spiritual lives in God's hands. We can rejoice when we have reached this point.

Then, as we begin to grow in love for the Lord and for our husbands, we may begin to see changes in our husbands. A man might be more open to meeting his wife's Christian friends or discussing what happens at prayer meetings. He might acknowledge that God might someday be a greater part of his life. The wife might feel an easing of tensions around the house or notice that they are both arguing less. We can rejoice in whatever glimmer of hope we notice. It is a sign that we have been following God's plan for our lives more faithfully than we used to. We should be glad that God is beginning to form us into holy women.

At the same time, however, we need to watch our imaginations. We can easily jump from a glimmer of hope to expecting that our husbands will want to be baptized in the Spirit right away. It seems that once our husbands begin opening up more to Jesus, all our good attitudes fly out the window. Once again, we find ourselves putting pressure on them or sharing too much. We get so excited inside that we can hardly think straight.

If we find this happening, we can go to Jesus, repent, and talk it over with him. He knows how badly we want our husbands to make a deeper commitment to him. He above all others can share in our pain, because he wants the same thing. We can trust that Jesus will put peace into our hearts and set our feet back on the right path.

We will probably experience this pattern of over-reacting to signs of change in our husbands many times as they mature in knowledge of Christ. We are not regressing each time; we are learning at different levels of our being.

The process can be compared to a ship going through the locks of a canal. At each level, the lock closes behind the ship. As water fills the lock, buoying the ship, it may cause some turbulence. But finally, the ship can move smoothly into the next lock. One lock may look a lot like another, so a passenger might not notice much progress. But the ship has reached a new level. It keeps going through the locks until eventually it leaves the canal for smoother sailing.

That is a good way to view difficulties we have in maintaining the right attitudes about our husbands. We cannot always see that we are making progress, but we are steadily moving forward each time we stumble, repent, and go on.

Two incidents helped me very much as I struggled through the locks. At one point after Russ had been baptized in the Spirit, I was becoming impatient with the pace of his growth as a Christian. Occasionally, I would share with another woman some of the things my husband had said or done which indicated how much he was growing. After I had done this several times, she very gently told me that she was not comfortable hearing about Russ's spiritual progress. I realized that my impatience showed that I still considered my husband less than a whole Christian and unable to function as I thought a head should.

Sometime after this, Russ and I faced some serious decisions about future directions for our life. I was afraid my husband would not accept the direction that I felt was right. I lacked trust that God would guide him to the best decision. Finally I talked to Russ and told him that for some reason I was fearful about his relationship with God. Bringing this fear into the light did a great deal to free me. Russ was able to encourage me—first by requesting that I continue to pray for him to become a strong and holy man of God, and then by reassuring me that Jesus was Lord of his life. There would be no turning back, no matter what direction God wanted us to take.

Not long after that I experienced a new problem. I realized my husband had been truly changed and molded by the Lord. I was thrilled to find this out, and immediately wanted the whole world to know. But the Lord told me that I did not have to advance my husband in the eyes of others. If he was really growing in the Lord, his life would begin bearing good fruit. I did not have to say anything.

All of these incidents showed me that I had a severe case of spiritual pride. It is as if I was waiting for Russ to "catch up" with me spiritually. Yet while it was true that in some ways I had experienced more Christian growth than Russ, in other ways I was miles behind him.

I have experienced all the wrong attitudes I have been talking about. Yet through it all, Jesus was loving me. He loved me while I held a wrong attitude, he loved me as I realized I needed to repent of that, and he loved me as I repented. He loved me as I allowed him to change my mind and heart, and he loved me when I did not realize that I needed more healing and changing. He still loves me now.

I know, too, that there's nothing special about me. Jesus loves you no less than me; he wants to purify you as well as me. We do not become purified overnight. But as we are being purified, let's remember that it is accomplished by Jesus who "died, or rather, was raised to life and is at the right side of God, pleading with him for us! For I am certain that nothing can separate us from his love; neither death nor life, neither angels nor other heavenly rulers or powers, neither the present nor the future, neither the world above nor the world below—

there is nothing in all creation that will ever be able to separate us from the love of God which is ours through Christ Jesus our Lord" (Rom. 8:34,38,39).

It is also reassuring to know that Russ did not wait until I was perfect to notice and respond to the fact I was changing. If that were true, he would still be waiting! Any change that takes place in our husbands' hearts is a work of the Holy Spirit. It is the Spirit who will stir up our husbands' hearts, melt them, and mold them. Our only responsibility is to keep our eyes on Jesus, allowing him to form us into holy women, as we pray for our husbands and children.

I would like to close this book with a prayer for you borrowed from Paul's letter to the Ephesians. This has been the prayer on my heart as I have sat here writing these past months.

I ask God from the wealth of his glory to give you power through his Spirit to be strong in your inner selves, and I pray that Christ will make his home in your hearts through faith. I pray that you may have your roots and foundation in love, so that you, together with all God's people, may have the power to understand how broad and long, how high and deep, is Christ's love. Yes, may you come to know his love—although it can never be fully known—and so be completely filled with the very nature of God.

To him who by means of his power working in us is able to do so much more than we can ever ask for, or even think of: to God be the glory in the church and in Christ Jesus for all time, forever and ever! Amen.

Eph. 3:16–21

APPENDIX

SERIOUS MARRIAGE PROBLEMS

> *Whoever comes to me cannot be my disciple unless he loves me more than he loves his father and his mother, his wife and his children, his brothers and his sisters, and himself as well. Whoever does not carry his own cross and come after me cannot be my disciple.*
>
> Luke 14:26–27

We must all count the cost of following Jesus. Becoming a Christian does not mean joining some sort of club in which we participate to the extent our other activities allow. Becoming Christian is learning a new way of life that demands total loyalty to the Lord, no matter what the cost.

In this book, we have talked about the high cost many wives pay in learning to be Christian wives to husbands who do not fully share their Christian commitment. Sometimes, when very serious problems are involved in the marriage, this cost may go beyond the sacrifice of pride or change of attitude that we have discussed. In some such cases, wives have been instrumental in bringing husbands out of real darkness—homosexuality, alcoholism, spiritism, adultery—into a relationship with Jesus. Yet some women, for whom the cost is just as high, do not see results in their marriages. Their husbands remain in darkness.

In extreme cases, the wife may have to leave her husband for a time especially if there is immediate physical danger to herself or to her children. In the most extreme cases, a husband may forbid the wife to be a Christian and insist that she join him in sins whose consequences are death to eternal life. Here the wife must count the cost: to live at any price with her husband now and to forsake the life of heaven, or to suffer the pain of leaving her husband and receive the hope of unending joy with Jesus.

The choices seem obvious, but the situations leading to them are seldom so clearly defined. Moreover, a woman may imagine that her situation is far worse than it is, because she lacks the courage to carry on. Or she could see a situation in a far more favorable light than is true.

It is clear in the Scriptures that Jesus wants husband and wife together (Matt. 19:3–9). Yet it is also true that if an unbelieving husband will not consent to his wife being a Christian, she may need to leave him (see 1 Cor. 7:10–16). Now the fact that your husband does not want you to attend weekly prayer meetings does not necessarily mean he is keeping you from being a Christian. There are occasional situations, however, where a husband will forbid his wife any relationship with Jesus and may insist she join him in some serious sin like witchcraft or partner switching. Obviously one cannot be a follower of Jesus and participate in these activities.

A woman who finds herself in such an extreme position with her husband should seek good Christian counsel from a mature, reliable person—perhaps her pastor or minister or a trusted Christian brother or sister.

It is important to stay with the counsel the Lord gives you. Advice hopping means you probably are not open to God's will for your life, but rather are seeking someone to say that you're right.

A woman caught in an extreme situation especially needs to remember that her place of refuge is with the Lord.

> Hear my cry, O God; listen to my prayer! In despair and far from home I call to you!
>
> Take me to a safe refuge, for you are my protector, my strong defense against my enemies.
>
> Let me live in your sanctuary all my life; let me find safety under your wings. You have heard my promises, O God, and you have given me what belongs to those who honor you.
>
> Psalm 61:1–5

> I depend on God alone; I put my hope in him. He alone protects and saves me; he is my defender, and I shall never be defeated. My salvation and honor depend on God; he is my strong protector; he is my shelter.
>
> Psalm 62:5–8

Go to him. Let him hide you in a cleft of the rock. One woman described to me her feelings as she struggled through a difficult time with her husband. He was an alcoholic and would become violent, so at times she would have to take her son and seek shelter elsewhere. When she would seek the Lord, she felt that she was hidden in a cave on the side of a mountain. Outside the shelter given her, she could see a violent storm raging with huge hailstones beating down. If she ventured out of her cave she became terribly hurt, so more and more she learned to accept the Lord's protection.

This protection is real. It is not withdrawal from life. It is, rather, the acknowledgement that life has become very difficult and that unless one seeks the Rock of refuge for protection, one could die.

I have included this brief mention of extreme marital situations in order not to burden a woman in such a situation with impossible talk about submission. Of course, one should be as loving and compassionate as possible, but God does not expect or want us to submit to sin: to submit to turning away from the One who is our life.

Also by Ruth Sanford

More than Survivors
God's Way of Restoration for Women

Encouragement and practical help for Christian women who want to overcome common personal problems to become the women God meant them to be. $4.95

By Therese Cirner
The Facts about Your Feelings
What Every Christian Woman Should Know

Offers insight and practical guidelines to help women understand, control, and creatively channel their emotions. A lifelong resource book for women of every age and background. Excellent both for personal use and for use by small groups. $4.95

By Elisabeth Elliot
The Savage My Kinsman

The true story in text and pictures of Elisabeth Elliot's venture into the territory of the Auca Indians of Ecuador—the savage tribe who murdered her missionary husband Jim Elliot. $5.95